FAVORITE JAPANESE DISHES

Distributed by JAPAN PUBLICATIONS TRADING CO., LTD

Distributors:

UNITED STATES: Kodansha America, Inc., through Oxford University Press, 198 Madison Avenue, New York, NY 10016

CANADA: Fitzhenry & Whiteside Ltd., 195 Allstate Parkway, Markham, Ontario L3R 4T8

UNITED KINGDOM AND EUROPE: Premier Book Marketing Ltd., Clarendon House, 52, Cornmarket Street, Oxford,OX1 3HJ England

AUSTRALIA AND NEW ZEALAND: Bookwise International, 174 Cormack Road, Wingfield, SA 5013 Australia

ASIA & JAPAN: Japan Publications Trading Co., Ltd., 1-2-1, Sarugaku-cho, Chiyoda-ku, Tokyo 101-0064 Japan

First Printing : July 2004

Original Copyright © 2004 by JOIE, INC.

ISBN4-88996-132-1

ACKNOWLEDGMENTS

We, the editors of JOIE, INC., wish to thank the following individuals who have been generous in helping us compile the necessary materials for this book:

Yukiko Moriyama, Editorial Adviser & Coordinator

Shiro Shimura, Akira Naito, Editorial Assistance

Yoichi Suzuki, Director of Photography

Mariko Suzuki, Illustrations

INTRODUCTION

Japanese cuisine is known around the world for its distinctive taste and appearance. Esthetically pleasing displays of the varied dishes are considered just as important as the food itself. The mood of the season can often be felt in the dishes, and they should give a sense of visual satisfaction. Each Japanese dish is artfully arranged in individual bowls, plates, and/or dishes for each person. Often, all courses are presented at one time and eaten in no particular order.

Japan is surrounded by the sea, and consists principally of four main islands. Her total size, location, and population, all combine to demand that much of the people's food come from the ocean, and her world roving fishing fleets supply that need admirably. It is estimated that the average Japanese consumes 70 lbs. (31.7 kg.) of seafood a year. Among the various methods of fish preparation, the most popular are to fry, or present them raw, as in *sashimi* or *sushi*. Perhaps *sushi*, bite-size pieces of fresh fish pressed onto a ball of vinegared rice, and *tempura*, shrimp and vegetables coated with an egg batter and deep-fried, are best known to Westerners. Meat dishes were introduced in the last century as a new "Western cuisine."

Japanese culinary tradition has been much influenced by that of Korea and China. Buddhism arrived via Korea in the 6th century, and the eating of meat was discouraged. Chopsticks and soy sauce came from China in the 8th century. The introduction to Japan of Zen Buddhism in the 13th century held as one of its tenets strict adherence to vegetarianism, and the consumption of meat was banned until about a hundred years ago. During the course of her long history, nearly every part of Japan developed its own delightful regional food specialties, and the people became skilled in preparing a number of beef dishes. *Sukiyaki* is one of the most widely enjoyed of such distinctive Japanese dishes. Today, Japanese restaurants are spreading throughout the United States, and the rest of the world. In spite of the fact that many people enjoy Japanese foods, they may be reluctant to try making them at home. Perhaps it is because they lack the knowledge and skills necessary, or feel hinderd by the limited availability of ingredients. Japanese cooking doesn't have to be a complicated task. There are many one-pot dishes, cooked at the table somewhat like fondue and these tend to create an intimate and cozy setting. Preparation orderly beforehand at the table of utensils and ingredients leaves you time to enjoy your company, rather than being stuck in the kitchen. With that idea in mind, emphasis throughout this book has been placed upon easy and efficient preparation of different dishes, along with serving suggestions and appropriate table etiquette where applicable. For the favorite dishes of *SHABU-SHABU, SUKIYAKI, TEMPURA, TEPPAN-YAKI,* and *TERIYAKI* the necessary ingredients are available either at large supermarkets, or oriental grocery stores. Also, we've listed as many substitutes as possible. To make these dishes enjoyable for everyone, each of the recipes has as many process pictures shown as possible, so that the directions can be followed easily, rather than having to depend entirely on written instructions. You can be assured of consistently good results. The following are explanations of the above mentioned dishes:

SHABU-SHABU: A dish consisting of paper thin sliced meat cooked in a stock with vegetables. Good quality meat is essential, and as it is thinly sliced, it takes only a few seconds to cook. *Shabu-shabu* is supposed to represent the sound of the simmering cooking stock being swished back and forth by a piece of meat which is held by chopsticks. The meat and vegetables are cooked according to the "drop-and-retrieve" method to the diners taste and dipping sauces are provided.

SUKIYAKI: This is one of Japan's best known dishes. It is somewhat similar to *Shabu-shabu*, but the main difference is in the cooking sauce. *Sukiyaki* is thinly sliced beef, generally sirloin tip, which is cooked in a broth of *dashi* stock (See p. 76), *sake* or *mirin* (Japanese sweet cooking wine), and/or sugar, with *tofu* and other vegetables. All diners serve themselves by taking what they want from the shallow, simmering cast-iron pan, and then dipping it into a bowl of beaten raw egg, which adds to the taste, and also helps to cool the food avoiding a burnt tongue. You may skip the raw egg if you wish. Hot rice served separately is the standard accompaniment.

TEMPURA: *Tempura* was first introduced to Japan by the Portuguese in the 16th century. *Tempura* is shrimp or prawns coated in a light, delicate batter made with egg, ice water, all-purpose flour and deep fried. To eat first dip into a mixture of soy sauce, *dashi* stock and grated *daikon* radish, a touch of chili pepper or lemon juice may be added if required.

TEPPAN-YAKI: Tenderloin or sirloin steak and vegetables are diced and cooked on a smooth, hot grill. Since everything is eaten with chopsticks, the meat and vegetables are cut into bite-size pieces for cooking. A *teppan-yaki* restaurant is a Japanese steak house. The chef cooks the meal on a hot, stainless steel grill right in front of you. The presentation is unique. Since beef is relatively new in Japanese cooking, some people consider this style of cooking as "Western cuisine".

TERIYAKI: The word *teriyaki* comes from *teri* (shiny or glazed), and *yaki* (grilled or broiled). The most popular meats, beef or chicken, are marinated in a mixture of soy sauce, *sake, mirin,* and/or sugar, grated ginger root, and garlic, then cooked either in a skillet or on a grill.

The editors of Joie, Inc. and I hope that this book will help you to enjoy the food as much as we have.

Tokyo, November 1986

Yukiko Moriyama

MA

Japan and

Location of Japan

Sea of J

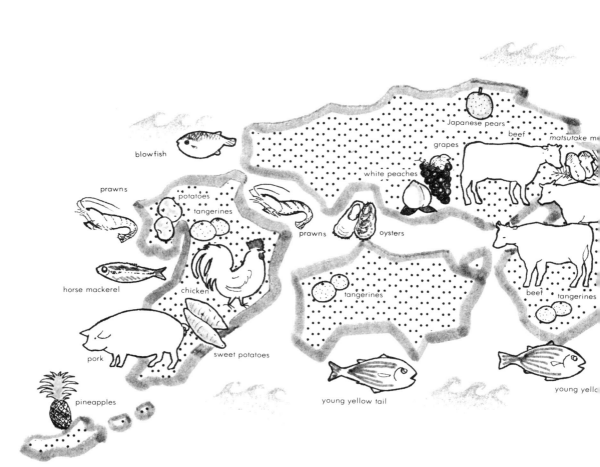

blowfish

prawns

potatoes

tangerines

white peaches

grapes

Japanese pears

beef

matsutake m

horse mackerel

chicken

prawns

oysters

tangerines

beef

tangerines

pork

sweet potatoes

young yellow tail

young yello

pineapples

JAPAN

ducts

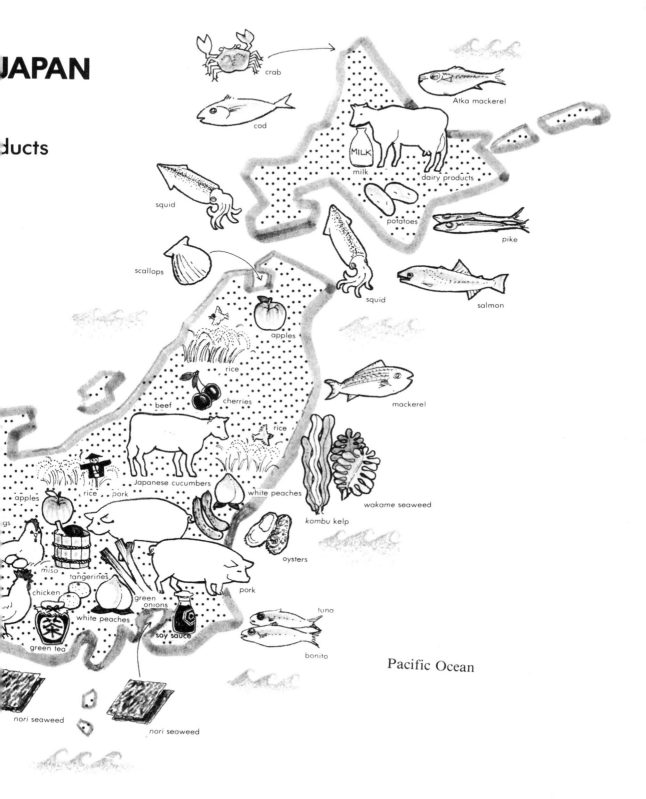

crab

cod

Atka mackerel

squid

MILK

milk

dairy products

potatoes

pike

scallops

squid

salmon

apples

rice

mackerel

beef

cherries

rice

Japanese cucumbers

white peaches

wakame seaweed

apples

rice

pork

kombu kelp

gs

miso

tangerines

oysters

chicken

green onions

pork

white peaches

soy sauce

tuna

green tea

bonito

Pacific Ocean

nori seaweed

nori seaweed

7

BASIC COOKING INFORMATION

★ 1 cup is equivalent to 240 ml in our recipes: (American cup measurement)
  1 American cup=240 ml=8 American fl oz
  1 British cup=200 ml=7 British fl oz
  1 Japanese cup=200 ml

1 tablespoon=15 ml   1 teaspoon=5 ml

	T=tablespoon	t=teaspoon	fl=fluid	oz=ounce	lb=pound
ml=milliliter	g=gram	in=inch	cm=centimeter	F=Fahrenheit	C=Celsius

TABLES CONVERTING FROM U.S. CUSTOMARY SYSTEM TO METRICS

Liquid Measures

U.S. Customary system	oz	g	ml
1/16 cup= 1 T	1/2 oz	14g	15ml
1/4 cup= 4 T	2 oz	60g	59ml
1/2 cup= 8 T	4 oz	115g	118ml
1 cup=16 T	8 oz	225g	236ml
1 3/4 cups	14 oz	400g	414ml
2 cups=1 pint	16 oz	450g	473ml
3 cups	24 oz	685g	710ml
4 cups	32 oz	900g	946ml

Liquid Measures

Japanese system	oz	ml
1/8 cup	7/8 oz	25ml
1/4 cup	1 3/4 oz	50ml
1/2 cup	3 1/2 oz	100ml
1 cup	7 oz	200ml
1 1/2 cups	10 1/2 oz	300ml
2 cups	14 oz	400ml
3 cups	21 oz	600ml
4 cups	28 oz	800ml

Weights

ounces to grams*
1/4 oz= 7g
1/2 oz= 14g
1 oz= 30g
2 oz= 60g
4 oz=115g
6 oz=170g
8 oz=225g
16 oz=450g

* Equivalent

Linear Measures

inches to centimeters
1/2 in= 1.27cm
1 in= 2.54cm
2 in= 5.08cm
4 in=10.16cm
5 in=12.7 cm
10 in=25.4 cm
15 in=38.1 cm
20 in=50.8 cm

Temperatures

Fahrenheit (F) to Celsius (C)		
freezer storage	−10°F=	−23.3°C
	0°F=	−17.7°C
water freezes	32°F=	0 °C
	68°F=	20 °C
	100°F=	38 °C
water boils	212°F=	100 °C
	300°F=	150 °C
	400°F=	204.4°C

Deep-Frying Oil Temperatures

300°F−330°F (150°C−165°C)=low
340°F−350°F (170°C−175°C)=moderate
350°F−360°F (175°C−180°C)=high

CONTENTS

SHABU-SHABU

SHABU-SHABU

The name arrives from the sound made when the meat is swished back and forth in the stock to cook. This dish belongs to *nabemono* in Japanese (or one-pot cooking). When it is placed in the center of the table, it creates a heart warming atmosphere for family anytime of the year, especially during winter. This style of eating originated in China, introduced to the northern Chinese by Muslim and Mongol traders, the special pot that we use for *shabu-shabu* is called the Peking Pot in China and has steadily gained popularity for its relaxed help yourself cooking style.

Use hot pot as a table center piece (See p 14–17), lay accordingly.

1 Have all ingredients and utensils ready + *sake*!

The authentic "shabu-shabu" or "Peking Pot" pans are ring shaped copper pans which hold charcoal in the center. Copper, stainless steel, flame proof casseroles or electric skillets make good substitutes.

For cooking at the table use a small burner capable of a high heat.

Place prepared meat (See p 14), vegetables (See p 15, 16), 2 kinds of sauces (See p 16), and 3 kinds of condiments (See p 17) within easy reach.

Provide individual bowls, chopsticks and ladles for skimming and serving soup.

2 Make the stock.

① Lightly wipe the surface of *kombu* kelp and line the pan. Add water to fill three quarters of the pan; turn on the heat.

② When water starts to bubble on bottom of the pan, lift *kombu* kelp out, and simmer gently.

3 Take sauces and condiments.

Choose your sauce and condiments.

Cook it yourself!

4 Start cooking/eating.

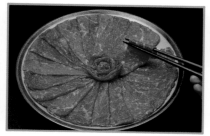

① Using chopsticks, take the meat first slice by slice.

② In the simmering stock, swish meat back and forth. Do not overcook.

③ When color of the meat turns pink, immediately transfer into dipping sauce with condiments.

④ Repeat processes 1–3. Carefully skim the stock.

⑤ Add vegetables of your choice. Take what is cooked.

5 For the second course, add noodles, rice cakes, or cooked rice.

● Noodles

Cook dried thick noodles as directed on package. Add to the *shabu-shabu* stock and simmer a few minutes. Dip into sauce and condiments of your choice.

● Rice Cakes

① Add rice cakes to the *shabu-shabu* stock and cook until soft.

② Dip into sauce and condiments of your choice.

● Rice

① Remove residue from the *shabu-shabu* stock. Transfer the clear stock to a small saucepan.

② Add cooked rice (hot or cold) and cook over medium heat. Bring to a boil, season to taste with salt and soy sauce; lower heat and gently pour in beaten eggs.

③ When the eggs start to set, remove from the heat and transfer into serving bowl(s). Garnish with trefoil or chives, if desired.

SHABU-SHABU

INGREDIENTS: 4–6 servings

21 oz (600g) beef loin or rump, sliced extremely fine
1/4 bunch or 18 oz (500g) Chinese cabbage
4 green onions
1/2 bunch or 2 oz (50g) chrysanthemum leaves
1 oz (30g) bean threads, dried
3 1/2 oz (100g) mushrooms
12 oz (340g) soft *tofu*
3 1/2 oz (100g) *enokitake* mushrooms
2   4 in (10cm) square *kombu* kelp

Dipping Sauces
Sesame Sauce
  5 T white sesame seeds
  1 clove garlic
  1/2 cup *dashi* stock (See p 76)
  1 T each white *miso*, *sake*, *mirin*, sesame
    oil
  2 t soy sauce
  1 t salt
  Dash chili pepper
Ponzu Vinegar Sauce
  6 T soy sauce
  5 T *ponzu* vinegar or lemon juice

Condiments
Daikon Oroshi (grated *daikon* radish)
Momiji Oroshi (grated *daikon* radish with chili)
Chopped Chives

* Have your butcher slice beef loin or rump very thinly using a slicer. Preferably divide each slice with cellophane wrap for easy handling.
* Substitute spinach for chrysanthemum leaves.
* When making sesame sauce, sesame paste can be used to save the time for grinding.
* Other dipping sauces: **Peanut Sauce**: Blend 5 T peanut butter, 5 T *dashi* stock, 3 T each soy sauce and sugar. *Miso* **Sauce**: Blend 3 T white *miso*, 2 T each *mirin* and *dashi* stock.

1 Arrange the meat.

 ### When using pre-sliced meat

① Have your butcher slice beef paper-thin (the thinner the better).

② Cut into eating size (approx 4 in, 10cm length).

 ### When using a cut of meat

① Thaw frozen meat slowly in refrigerator until the center 1/2 in (1.5cm) remain frozen.

② Using a sharp knife, carefully slice very finely across the grain.

To Arrange

① On 10 in (25cm) plate, arrange the slices one by one, so that diners can easily pick up. Fold the edges under overlapping slightly with each other in all directions, for fine presentation.

② Make a "rose" with meat in the center.

Beef for *Shabu-shabu*

Beef quality depends on the cow's age, grade and method of breeding. Japanese beef is said to be the best quality in the world, it's reared on beer especially "Matsuzaka beef" from Mie prefecture, "Kobe beef" from Hyogo prefecture and "Yonezawa beef" from Yamagata prefecture. For *shabu-shabu* the most recommendable part is loin roast. Loin roast taken from the back rib, has an excellent flavor with balanced fat and the lean which we call "marbling". If this is too expensive, substitute with round of beef.

2 Prepare vegetables.

 ### Chinese Cabbage

① Remove core at the base. Pull off leaves, wash each leaf under running water; drain.

② Separate leaf part and stem part as their cooking time differ.

③ Cut leaf and stem apart.

④ Pare the stem part to enlarge the cut side.

⑤ Cut the leaf part a little larger than stem for easy cooking.

 ### Green Onions

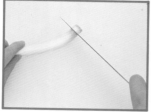   

① Wash carefully under running water. Remove dirty skin at the root end.

② Cut off dirty or discolored part of green section.

③ Cut white part into 3/8 in (1 cm) diagonal slices.

④ Cut green part into 2 in (5 cm).

Chrysanthemum Leaves (or spinach)

① Wash carefully. To remove dirt at the root ends and between leaves and stems, shake in water one by one.

② Remove discolored or withered leaves.

③ Discard tough stems.

④ Cut into 2 in (5 cm) length.

 ### Bean Threads

   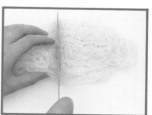

① Add bean threads in boiling water.

② Allow to soften until transparent, approx 2–3 minutes.

③ Drain in a strainer.

④ When cooled, cut 2–3 places in both directions for easy handling.

SHABU-SHABU

 Mushrooms (*Shiitake* mushrooms are shown here)

 Tofu

① Look for firm, fresh-looking ones. Trim away hard stem ends. If using dried *shiitake* mushrooms, soak in lukewarm water (See p 77).

② Fillip dust from underside. Wash only dirty ones. Pat dry.

③ Make a decorative cut on the caps.

Cut *tofu* into 1 in (2.5 cm) cubes.

 Enokitake Mushrooms

 To Arrange

① Hold at the ends and wash in water to remove dirt.

② Cut off discolored ends, approx 1 in (2.5 cm); discard.

Have a large plate. Arrange Chinese cabbage, green onions, chrysanthemum leaves, bean threads, mushrooms and *tofu* coordinating colors.

3 Make dipping sauces.

 Sesame Sauce

① Skin garlic clove; clean.

② Pat dry and slice thinly.

③ Crush garlic in mortar with pestle.

④ Add sesame seeds (roasted) and grind until creamy.

⑤ Add remaining ingredients and blend well.

 Ponzu Sauce

 To Arrange

In a bowl add soy sauce and vinegar or lemon juice, blend well.

In sauce pots, pour each sauce and provide serving spoons.

Quick & Easy Shabu-shabu Sauces

The secret of *shabu-shabu* lies not only in the quality of beef but also in the fine flavor of the sauce. It is best to make your own sauces but if you are a beginner, commercial sauces are adequate. There are several types available and it's a good idea to keep some in stock for emergencies, then add your own seasonings to enjoy *shabu-shabu*.

4 Prepare condiments.

 Daikon Oroshi

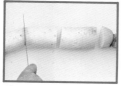 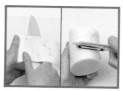   

① Wash *daikon* radish and pat dry. Cut off 1 in (2.5cm) from stem end and cut remaining into 2 or 3 pieces.

② Peel with a peeler.

③ Grate. If using food processor, cut into chunks and work at medium speed.

④ When the radish is too small to grate, use it to scrape off the grated radish between 'teeth'.

⑤ Place onto a bamboo mat or a strainer and allow to drain.

 Momiji Oroshi

① Wash 3-4 hot red peppers. Remove stems and seeds.

② If the peppers are very dry, soak in water with 1-2 drops of vinegar until softened.

③ Wash *daikon* radish and pat dry. Cut off 1 in (2.5cm) from the stem and cut remaining into 2-3.

④ Peel with a peeler.

⑤ Thrust a chopstick into the cut side and make holes for each pepper.

⑥ Insert chopstick into seeded hot red pepper and thrust into the hole.

⑦ Using a fine grater, grate the pepper side. Work slowly and carefully so as not to make large flakes of pepper.

⑧ Place onto bamboo mat or a strainer and allow to drain.

Momiji Oroshi

Daikon radish is grated together with hot red pepper to add hotness to *daikon oroshi*. Its scarlet tinted transparency resembles autumnal maple leaves, hence the name. Carrot is also used for this effect. *Momiji oroshi* is an essential condiment in light-flavored *nabemono* dishes such as *shabu-shabu, chiri-nabe, mizutaki* (See p 82). It is always mixed into *ponzu* vinegar sauce. It is also served as a garnish for fried fish which has rather a light flavor. When grating, use a fine grater and work against the grain.

 Chopped Chives

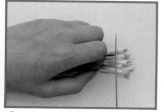 

① Lightly wash and pat dry. Remove the root and withered leaves.

② Holding 7-8 stalks, slice finely. Place in a tiny bowl.

 To Arrange

Place drained *daikon oroshi, momiji oroshi,* and chopped chives shaping into mounds.

Now preparation is done. Let's enjoy eating following the eating directions on page 12, 13.

SHABU-SHABU

This dish owns another name — "Habitual Hot Pot" as it is sometimes called, because nobody gets tired of the delicious taste even if it is served every evening. The difference from the beef *shabu-shabu* is to cook the pork thoroughly.

INGREDIENTS: 4-6 servings

14 oz (400g) pork loin, sliced very thin
7 oz (200g) spinach
4 in (10cm) square *kombu* kelp

Dipping Sauce
Ginger Sauce
{ 4 T soy sauce
{ 1 T *mirin*
{ 2 t grated fresh ginger

Condiments
Momiji Oroshi (grated *daikon* radish with chili)
Chopped Chives

1 Prepare meat.

Slice half-frozen pork paper-thin or ask your butcher to do it. Cut into bite-size pieces. Arrange each slice attractively on a plate.

2 Prepare spinach.

① Shake spinach in water to remove dirt, holding root ends.

② Cut off roots.

③ Cut into bite-size pieces and drain in colandar. Arrange on a plate, separating leaves and stalks if possible.

3 Make *dashi* stock.

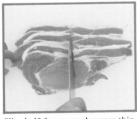

① Wet *kombu* kelp and rub with dry towel to remove grit and dirt.

② Fill serving pot with water about ½ way and add *kombu* kelp.

③ Let stand 30–40 minutes.

4 Make dip.

Ginger Sauce

Mix all sauce ingredients and pour into a deep bowl. Provide a spoon for serving.

5 Prepare condiments.

 Momiji Oroshi

  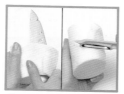  

① Wash 3–4 hot red peppers and discard stems and seeds.

② If the peppers are very dry, soak in water with 1–2 drops of vinegar until softened.

③ Wash *daikon* radish and pat dry. Cut off green top for 1 in (2.5cm) and peel the remainder. Cut into 2–3, to grate.

④ Plug a chopstick into the cut side and make holes for each hot red pepper.

⑤ Insert a chopstick into seeded hot red pepper and thrust into the hole.

⑥ Using a fine grater, grate the pepper side. Work slowly and carefully so as not to make large flakes of pepper.

⑦ Transfer onto a bamboo mat or a strainer. Let stand to drain. Place in a small dish.

 Chopped Chives

① Wash briefly and pat dry. Remove roots and discolored leaves.

② Holding 7–8 stalks together, slice very finely. Transfer to a small dish.

Now the table is perfect. Gather round and "dig in".

① Bring the stock in the pot to a boiling point; take out *kombu* kelp.

② Spread pork slices into the stock, one by one. Cook the only amount that the diners can eat at once.

③ Skim off residue carefully.

④ Cook spinach root ends first. Add the leaves later as they cook quickly.

⑤ When the pork changes its color and shrinks, it is ready to eat.

⑥ Put dipping sauce and favorite condiments in each serving bowl. Dilute the sauce with simmering stock, if desired.

⑦ Do not overcook. Cook the remainder when everything is taken out from the pot, adding a small portion at a time.

SHABU-SHABU

Another version of beef *shabu-shabu*. Chicken and vegetables are cooked in rich chicken stock, creating a one-pot dish to enjoy. Dip into *ponzu* vinegar sauce and/or seasame sauce (See p 16).

INGREDIENTS: 4–6 servings

14 oz (400g) chicken thigh (with skin)
4 oz (115g) chrysanthemum leaves
3½ oz (100g) mushrooms
20 oz (570g) *shirataki* filaments
Soup
{ 2 chicken bones
{ 8 cups water
{ Leftover vegetables (onion, carrot)
Dipping Sauce
Miso Sauce
{ 3 white *miso*
{ 2 T each *mirin* and *dashi* stock (p76)
Condiment
Chopped Chives

1 Make the chicken stock.

① Look for well cleaned chicken bones. Chop into pieces to place in a saucepan.

② In boiling water, blanch chicken bones to remove odor; rinse in cold water.

③ In a saucepan add water, leftover bits of vegetables, and bones. Cook over medium heat.

④ When boiling, remove residue and reduce heat. Simmer 2–3 hours.

⑤ Strain and fill a serving pot to 70% full.

2 Prepare the meat.

   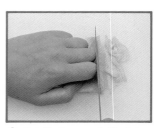

① Separate chicken flesh and skin. Insert a knife between skin and flesh. Pulling the skin with your left fingers, peel off the skin working the knife back and forth.

② Slice the flesh as thin as possible.

③ Blanch the skin in boiling water and turn into cold water. This makes the skin tender and 'crunchy', and also removes the odor.

④ Cut the layers of skin into ¼ in (¾cm) wide strips.

3 Prepare the vegetables.

 Chrysanthemum Leaves

① Shake off dirt in water carefully. Remove yellow or withered leaves.

② Trim away hard stems. Cut into 2 in (5cm) length. If chrysanthemum leaves are unobtainable, spinach can be substituted.

 Mushrooms (*Shiitake* mushrooms)

① Look for the same large size. Trim away brown ends of stem. Wash briefly and pat dry.

② Make a decorative cut on the caps.

 Shirataki Filaments

① Wash and drain. Cook briefly in boiling water to remove harsh taste.

② Drain in a colander.

③ Cut into 3 in (8cm).

4 Arrange.

Arrange chicken, chrysanthemum leaves, mushrooms and *shirataki* filaments attractively on a plate.

5 Make dipping sauce.

 Miso Sauce

① In a small saucepan, add all *miso* sauce ingredients.

② Cook and stir over low heat until thickened. Allow to cool. Transfer to a small bowl and serve with a spoon.

6 Prepare condiment.

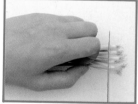 Chopped Chives

① Wash lightly and pat dry. Remove roots and discolored leaves.

② Holding 7–8 stalks together, slice very finely. Transfer to a small dish.

Now the table is perfectly set. Sit around the pot and start!

① Bring the stock in the pot to a boil. Add *shirataki* filaments, mushrooms, and then chicken slices.

② When chicken changes color, add chrysanthemum leaves.

③ Pour dipping sauce and condiment in each bowl and dip cooked food.

SUKIYAKI

SUKIYAKI

Sukiyaki actually translates as "Hoe grilling" (See explanation p 29). A type of barbecue which was introduced to Japan during the last century. It is classified as a *nabemono* however the cooking method differs and the taste is richer. Beef is first grilled in an iron pan and then cooked in *warishita* (*sukiyaki* cooking sauce) with vegetables. This easy and tasty dish is now loved throughout the world!

Prepare and lay the table (See p 26–29) and "tuck in"!

1 Have all the necessary items ready.

The average *sukiyaki* pan is a flat bottomed iron one, approx 3 in (8 cm) deep. A heavy non-stick pan or thick based skillet may be substituted. If using an iron pan, fill with water and bring to a boil, discard water and heat dry. Pour in some oil and heat rotating the pan. The oil will be absorbed by the pan and prevent sticking. After each usage pat completely dry to avoid rust.

Arrange plates of meat (See p 26), vegetables (See p 27–28), and sauce (See p 29) on the table with individual dishes, chopsticks and eggs.

2 Now start cooking.

① Preheat pan well. Add beef suet and rub into the sides and bottom of pan.

② Spreading the slices, add beef and briefly cook both sides.

③ Pour in *warishita* to cover the meat. Bring to a boil.

④ Immediately add vegetables which require longer cooking time. Add only a portion that can be eaten at a time.

3 Have your egg ready.

① Let each diner break an egg into individual bowl.   ② Beat lightly.

4 Let's eat.

When meat changes color, take out. Dip into beaten egg and eat. To avoid overcooking, take out everything before adding further ingredients and *warishita*.

5 Shall we top off with rice or noodles?

⬤ Noodles

Add cooked noodles and bring to a boil. Adjust the taste of sauce by adding *dashi* stock first, then soy sauce.

⬤ Rice

Add cooked rice and simmer until it absorbs the taste of sauce. Adjust the taste with soy sauce or *dashi* stock. Stir in beaten egg.

How about a change?

Think of the diners taste, the season, and of course your budget and make your own assortment. Ingredients may be presented on individual plats so the diners can recognize his or her preference.

SUKIYAKI

INGREDIENTS: 4–6 servings

21 oz (600 g) beef loin or round, sliced very thin
18 oz (500 g) Chinese cabbage (¼ head)
4 green onions
4 oz (115 g) chrysanthemum leaves
20 oz (570 g) *shirataki* filaments
8 *shiitake* mushrooms
12 oz (340 g) grilled *tofu*
3½ oz (100 g) *enokitake* mushrooms
Warishita (sukiyaki) cooking sauce)
⎧ ½ cup *dashi* stock (See p 76)
⎨ 3 T each soy sauce and *mirin*
⎩ 1 T each sugar and *sake*
Beef suet
4 eggs

* If chrysanthemum leaves or other Japanese ingredients are unobtainable, substitute as follows:
Chrysanthemum leaves: spinach (parboiled)
Fresh *shiitake* mushrooms: button mushrooms (sliced)

1 Prepare the meat.

 Sliced Beef

 Beef Cut

Cut the thin slices into eating pieces, approx 4 in (10 cm) length.

① If using frozen beef cut, slowly thaw until it's still frozen in the center about 1 in (2.5 cm).

② Using a sharp knife, slice very thinly, against the grain.

 To Arrange

On a 8 in (20 cm) plate, place each slice of beef so that diners can take it easily. Place 1 in (2.5 cm) cube beef suet.

Beef Cuts You Should Know

Chuck: Shoulder meat including most of neck, parts about the shoulder blade, and those about the first three ribs.

Tongue: An elastic texture is prized when grilled. Good for *teriyaki*.

Brisket, Neck: Less quality, but inexpensive.

Rib: Meat of ribs, in layers of fat and meat. Good for *teppan-yaki*, *teriyaki*, *sukiyaki*.

Loin Roasts: Thick and wide meat on back ribs. Fatty loin makes a good *sukiyaki* or *shabu-shabu*.

Fillet: The best quality beef for its tenderness and leanness. Good for *teppan-yaki* or *teriyaki*.

Rump: Rather tough meat of thigh. Good for *teriyaki*.

Round: Lean meat of thigh, cooked in various ways. Good for *teriyaki*.

Shank: Toughest meat. Good for simmered dishes.

Flank: This leaner meat should not be overcooked. Good for *shabu-shabu*.

2 Prepare vegetables.

 Chinese Cabbage

① Remove core and wash leaves one by one; drain.

② Separate leaf part and stem part as their cooking time differ. Cut them apart.

③ Leaf part and stem part are separated.

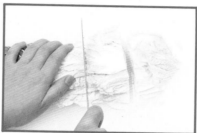

④ Pare the stem part slicing diagonally to enlarge the cut side. This helps the sauce penetrate effectively.

⑤ Cut leaf part into larger size as it cooks easily.

Chinese Cabbage

Annual or biannual plant of rape family, native to China.
Nutrition: Rich in vitamin C and other minerals.
To select: Take firm, heavy heads of fresh green and white cut edges. It is best to buy a whole head as half or quarter cuts do not keep well.

 Green Onions

① Wash thoroughly. Remove brown part at the root.

② Remove discolored or outer layers of the green.

③ Cut white part into ⅜ in (1 cm) diagonally.

④ Cut green part into 2 in (5 cm) length.

Chrysanthemum Leaves

① Wash carefully. To remove dirt at the root ends and between leaves and stems, shake in water, one at a time.

② Remove discolored or withered leaves.

③ Discard tough end of stem.

④ Cut into 2 in (5 cm) length.

SUKIYAKI

 ## Shirataki Filaments

① Wash and drain. Briefly cook in boiling water to remove harshness.

② Drain in a colander.

③ Cut into 3 in (8 cm).

Shiitake Mushrooms (Substitute with button mushrooms)

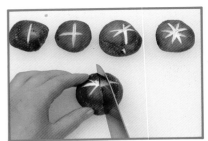

① Look for firm, same large size. Remove stems. (If using button mushrooms trim away brown ends of stem.)

② Fillip dust from underside. Wash only dirty ones. Pat dry.

③ Make a decorative cut on the caps. Slant the knife to make incisions.

Grilled Tofu

① In a colander, place grilled tofu. Pour over boiling water to clean; let stand to drain.

② Cut into 1 in (2.5 cm) cubes.

 ## To Arrange

Enokitake Mushrooms

① Holding at ends, whisk in water to remove dirt.

② Cut off discolored ends, for about 1 in (2.5 cm); discard.

Have a large plate. Arrange Chinese cabbage, green onions, chrysanthemum leaves, shirataki filaments, mushrooms, grilled tofu in heap attractively. Moist ingredients such as tofu and shirataki filaments are best served on a separate plate.

28

Preparation

3 Make *warishita* (*sukiyaki* cooking sauce).

Combine all ingredients in a small saucepan and bring to a boil. Simmer a few minutes to evaporate alcohol. Allow to cool; transfer to a sauce pot.

Quick & Easy Warishita

In *Kanto* area (eastern part of Japan), a prepared cooking sauce called *warishita* is used. It calls for some experience to make. We suggest that you try a commercial *warishita*, if you are a beginner. There are good professional *warishita* sauces readily available. Use it for a base and adjust to your taste.

Now the preparation is done. Start *sukiyaki* dinner as directed on page 24, 25!

Sukiyaki History

Nowadays *sukiyaki*, *sushi* and *tempura* are internationally renowned, however few people are aware of their origins. During the *Edo* period (17th century) meat was actually taboo, though records show that *sukiyaki* existed then. People hesitated to cook meat at home with their everyday cook ware. So they "cooked out", using farmers' tools such as the "*suki*" or "*kuwa*" (kind of shovel). They went out and cooked the catch of the day on the clean "*suki*" or "*kuwa*" and "*yaki*" means broiled, hence the name "*sukiyaki*" or so it is said.

There are other theories such as "paring meat thinly" "*suku*", but judging from most documents, the shovel of "*suki*" seems the most accurate.

Sukiyaki-Kanto style & Kansai style

Food custom differ according to the areas, even in Japan. *Sukiyaki* is cooked differently in *Kanto* (eastern Japan) and *Kansai* (western Japan).

In *Kanto* a light flavored cooking sauce called *warishita* is preferred, made with *dashi* stock, sugar, *sake* and soy sauce to braise the meat and vegetables. It is lightened or diluted with *dashi* stock for the individual's taste.

In *Kansai* sugar and soy sauce are added directly to the ingredients, 1/2 T sugar to 1 T soy sauce per 3 oz (100g) ratio of meat. For the sweet toothed add an extra bit of sugar. First cook the meat, then sprinkle with sugar and when it's absorbed add soy sauce. Bring to a boil. Then add the remaining ingredients. When the sauce becomes too thin, add *yakifu* (a spongy wheat gluten bread) to absorb excess moisture. When the sauce gets too thick, most ingredients, such as *tofu*, *shirataki* filaments and vegetables are added. It may be interesting to note, that vegetables in *Kanto* are called "*zaku*" accordingly to the sound made when chopping "*zaku zaku*—roughly.'' Whereas in *Kansai* they are called "*ashirai*" or "fancy garnish" or accompaniment.

29

SUKIYAKI   BEEF AND POTATOES

Do not throw away *sukiyaki* sauce! Leftover *sukiyaki* cooking sauce has concentrated flavors from all ingredients. So use it to create other dishes. Here potatoes are added to leftover *sukiyaki* to make a nutritious simmered dish which is often cooked in Japanese homes.

INGREDIENTS: 4 servings

7 oz (200g) leftover *sukiyaki*
3 medium potatoes (1 lb/450g)
Cooking Sauce
{ 2 cups *dashi* stock (See p 76)
{ 2 T soy sauce
{ 1 T sugar

* Taste when *sukiyaki* is added. If too light, add more seasonings such as soy sauce, sugar, *mirin*. If too thick, dilute with *dashi* stock.

1 Prepare potatoes.

① Wash potatoes and peel.

② Remove eyes.

③ Cut into 6–8 pieces.

④ Soak in cold water to extract over-strong flavor.

2 Let's cook.

① Bring cooking sauce ingredients and potatoes to a boil. Cook over moderate heat to retain the shape.

② Occasionally shake the pan or spoon over the cooking sauce and cook until a skewer can be inserted smoothly.

③ Add remainder of *sukiyaki* and stir gently so as not to break the potatoes. Bring to a boil; remove from heat.

SUKIYAKI — *GYUDON* (BEEF BOWL)

Easy but tasty lunch using leftover *sukiyaki*. Cold *sukiyaki* is turned into a delicious topping for hot cooked rice, by adding eggs. Add more beef for a more filling dish.

INGREDIENTS: 4 servings

6 cups cooked rice (See p 74)
11 oz (315g) leftover *sukiyaki*
4 eggs
8–10 stalks trefoil or coriander (optional)

* If leftover *sukiyaki* is not enough, adjust the amount by adding more vegetables such as sliced onion, spinach, celery.
* Adjust the taste when leftover *sukiyaki* is heated. If too light, add sugar, soy sauce, *mirin*. If too thick, dilute with *dashi* stock.
* *Sukiyaki* can be warmed and placed on hot cooked rice with left-over sauce without eggs.

1 Prepare topping.

❶ Wash trefoil and remove roots. Cut into 1 1/2 in (4cm) length.

❷ Beat eggs in a small bowl.

❸ Heat leftover *sukiyaki* on medium heat. When boiling, pour over beaten eggs evenly.

❹ When eggs are half-set, sprinkle with trefoil and remove from heat.

2 Let's arrange.

❶ In each serving bowl, heap hot cooked rice (about 1 1/2 cups).

❷ Place topping over rice and pour over cooking sauce.

Gyudon (Beef Bowl)

There is a *gyudon* boom in Japan, and you can find chain stores. This easy version of *sukiyaki* rice won massive popularity, especially among youngsters.

Ingredients (4 servings):
Cooked rice (See p 74)   10 1/2 oz (300 g) beef rib, sliced thin   1 medium onion, sliced thin   Cooking Sauce: [1 cup *dashi* stock (See p 76)   1/2 cup soy sauce   3 T sugar   2 T *mirin*   1 T *sake*]

Directions: Cut beef into bite-size pieces. Combine sauce ingredients in a saucepan, add beef and onion and cook until onion is transparent. In serving bowl place hot cooked rice and top with above.

SUKIYAKI

Same as an authentic *sukiyaki* except for the use of ground meat with beaten eggs. Prepare an extra cooking sauce as the ground meat is highly absorbent.

INGREDIENTS: 4–6 servings

14 oz (400g) ground beef
{ 1 egg
{ 1 t *sake*
4 oz (115g) spinach
4 green onions
3½ oz (100g) *shimeji* mushrooms
10 oz (285g) *shiraktaki* filaments
Warishita (*sukiyaki* cooking sauce)
{ 1½ cup *dashi* stock (See p 76) o
{   water
{ ½ cup each soy sauce and *mirin*
{ 3 T each sugar and *sake*
Beef suet
4 eggs

* Button mushrooms may be used in place of *shimeji* mushrooms.
* *Konnyaku* (devil's tongue) strips may be used in place of *shirataki* filaments.

1 Prepare meat.

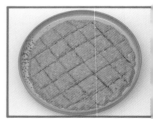

① Place ground meat in a bowl and add beaten egg and *sake*. Mix well with fingers until sticky.

② Spread on serving plate.

③ For easy handling, score in both directions.

④ Adequate serving size is about 1 in (2.5cm) per portion.

2 Prepare vegetables.

 Spinach

 Green Onions

① Holding root ends, shake off dirt in water.

② Trim away roots and cut into pieces. Drain in a colander.

① Wash and remove discolored part at root ends and green. Cut white part diagonally into ⅜ in (1cm).

② Cut green part into 2 in (5cm) length.

GROUND BEEF *SUKIYAKI*

 Shirataki Filaments

① Wash and drain. Cook briefly in boiling water to remove harsh taste.

② Drain in a colander. Cut into 3 in (8 cm).

Shimeji Mushrooms

① Trim away stem ends. Wash quickly in cold salted water; drain.

② Tear into bite-size pieces. If using button mushrooms, slice thinly.

 To Arrange

Arrange spinach, green onions, mushrooms attractively in heap on a dish, except *shirataki* filaments which have been cooked in advance.

3 Make *warishita*.

Bring all the ingredients to a boil, vaporizing the alcohol from the *sake* and *mirin*. Allow to cool and turn into a sauce pan.

Now the table is perfectly set. Let's sit around the pot and start *sukiyaki* dinner.

① Heat table pan (ideally cast iron pan) well. Melt beef suet and grease all sides.

② Cook and stir *shirataki* filaments on medium heat.

③ Pour in ⅓ amount of *warishita*.

④ When the sauce becomes bubbly, add ground beef in small portion carefully so as not to break up the shape.

⑤ Add vegetables.

⑥ Beat an egg in each serving bowl. Dip what is cooked and eat. When the sauce decreases, add more *warishita*.

SUKIYAKI

A variety of marinated seafood is cooked as for *sukiyaki* though this style has an even richer piquant sauce.

| INGREDIENTS: 4 servings |

2 fillets (14 oz/400g) white meat fish, cod or seabream
2 fillets (14 oz/400g) yellowtail
1 squid (10 oz/400g)
4 scallops
18 oz (500g) Chinese cabbage
10 oz (285g) *konnyaku* (devil's tongue) strips
4 oz (115g) *shimeji* mushrooms
1 bunch green onion

Warishita (*sukiyaki* cooking sauce)
1¾ cups water
6 T soy sauce
6 T *mirin*
1 T sugar

* Button mushrooms can be used in place of *shimeji* mushrooms.

1 Make *warishita* (*sukiyaki* cooking sauce).

Combine all ingredients well.

Warishita Sauce Pot

Nabemono, hot pot dishes such as *sukiyaki*, basically only need one large pot for cooking. But Japanese people enjoy collecting small tools such as sauce pots or condiment servers.

Sauce pots are very convenient tools when serving one-pot dishes. They are used for cooking sauce or *dashi* stock to thin. China ones with wide spouts are the most practical and popular. It is wise to choose one with a wide spout for easy care. Lacquer ware or glass ones are more elegant. Sometimes Japanese people use *sake* decanters.

2 Prepare seafood.

 Fish

Wash quickly in cold water and pat dry. Cut into bite-size slices, slanting knife.

> ### To Select Seafood for *Sukiyaki*
>
> Seafood *sukiyaki* was created by fishermen who cooked their day's catch in *sukiyaki* fashion on the boats. So it is important to look for very fresh ingredients.
> **Seabream:** White meat fish with a light flavor
> **Yellowtail:** Fatty fish loved by Japanese because it changes its name in each stage of growth, which means "promotion" or a successful life. It is rich in protein, vitamins and minerals.
> **Prawn or shrimp:** Look for live ones if possible, otherwise ones with heads still attached and looks transparent. Always remove veins.
> **Crab:** Fresh crabs have stretching tight legs and flexible shells. Crab gives zestful aroma to the broth as well as to the eye.

 Squid

① Separate the joint of body and tentacles with your fingers.

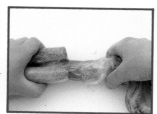
② Gently pull out tentacles.

③ Entrails follow. Do not break the ink bag.

④ Cut entrails off, discard.

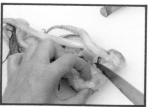
⑤ Slit the base open flat and remove beaks in the ball.

⑥ Remove eyes. Work in water as it may splash.

⑦ Using tip of knife, scrape off suckers for a better texture.

⑧ Tear off triangular "hat" with your fingers.

⑨ On top of the "hat", make a shallow cut to catch the skin. Peel off skin.

⑩ Insert knife into the body, cut the back to flatten.

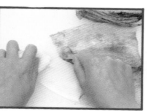
⑪ Using a cloth, rub the top to catch the skin; peel.

⑫ Carefully peel the skin.

SUKIYAKI

⑬ Cut off tough end; discard.

⑭ Slanting knife, score the surface on peeled side, in diamond pattern.

⑮ Cut into 1 in (2.5 cm) strips.

 Scallops

Wash quickly in salted water and pat dry. Remove dark entrails.

3 Marinate seafood.

In a deep dish or a baking pan, place fish, squid and scallops. Pour a quarter of *warishita* over evenly.

4 Prepare vegetables.

Chinese Cabbage

① Remove core and wash leaves one by one; drain.

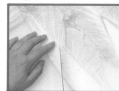

② Separate leaf and stem part as their cooking time differs. Cut them apart.

③ Leaf part and stem part are separated.

④ Pare the stem part, slanting knife.

⑤ Cut leaf part into larger size as it cooks quickly.

Konnyaku Strips

① Wash and cook in boiling water briefly to remove harsh taste.

② Drain in a colander. Cut into bite-size length.

Shimeji Mushrooms

① Trim away root ends. Shake off dirt in lightly salted water; drain.

② Tear into eating pieces. If using button mushrooms, slice thinly.

Green Onions

 To Arrange

Wash and pat dry. Remove root ends and cut into 2 in (5 cm) length.

Have a rather deep dish. Arrange Chinese cabbage, *konnyaku* strips, mushrooms and green onions attractively in heap.

The table's laid, get together and start your seafood *sukiyaki* dinner.

❶ In a serving pot, add remaining *warishita* and heat over medium heat. Add marinated seafood in small portions. Bring to a boil and skim residue.

❷ Add all *konnyaku* strips.

❸ Bring to a boil again and taking everyone's favorite morsel accompanied by the sauce.

❹ Add vegetables in small portions each time.

TEMPURA

Prawn

Sillago

Squid

Eggplant

Shishito Pepper

Green *Shiso* Leaf

TEMPURA   **Serve piping hot !**

Tempura consists of a rich variety of seafoods (mainly prawns) and vegetables, battered and deep fried. The batter which seals in the taste and the nutrients, is made simply with flour, egg and water. This dish must be served hot almost immediately from the pan and eaten by dipping into a special sauce (*tentsuyu*) and condiments or simply with lemon juice and salt.

Have everything on the table "ready and waiting" for the just-fried *tempura* (See p 41–47).

1 Place *tentsuyu*, condiments and utensils on the table.

The diner takes his condiments to mix with the *tentsuyu* (*tempura* dipping sauce), choosing from: *Daikon oroshi* (grated *daikon* radish) helping digest the oily *tempura*, grated ginger which whets the appetite for its pungency and fragrance. *Momiji oroshi* (grated *daikon* radish with chili) which enhances the light taste of fish. Be careful it's very hot!!! Other condiments are shredded green *shiso* leaves, *sansho* pepper, seven spice powder, shredded *nori* seaweed, chopped green onions, *kinome* sprigs.

2 Let's enjoy piping hot *tempura*.

Dip into *tentsuyu* sauce and eat immediately. Do not soak in sauce until *tempura* coating 'weeps'.

Tempura-A Brief History

Nowadays *tempura* is a No. 1 national dish and the origins can be traced to the 15th century, Japan's *Muromachi* period (14–16th century) when Portugese traders first introduced their cuisine and later combined it with Japanese and Chinese dishes, creating *tempura*.
Being considered an ethnic dish it did not gain popularity until the *Edo* period (17th century) when street vendors started selling it. By the turn of the period it had established itself as a main dinner feature.

INGREDIENTS: 4 servings

8 prawns or shrimps
4 sillago
1 squid
1 small eggplant
8 *shishito* or 2 green bell peppers
4 green *shiso* leaves
Flour for dusting
{ ¾ cup all-purpose flour
{ ⅔ cup ice water
{ 1 egg yolk
Oil for frying (to fill 80% of pan)
***Tentsuyu* (*tempura* dipping sauce)**
{ ¾ cup water
{ ¼ cup each dried bonito flakes, *mirin*,
{ soy sauce
Condiments
Daikon Oroshi (grated *daikon* radish)
Momiji Oroshi (grated *daikon* radish with chili)
Grated Ginger

1 Do the preparation.

 Prawn

① Wash and pat dry. Holding at the joint of head, pull the head off; devein.

② If using live or very fresh prawn, twist the head off, and the vein follows it.

③ If using head-off prawn, remove vein inserting a skewer into back.

④ Soak prawns in salted iced water 30 minutes to tighten the flesh.

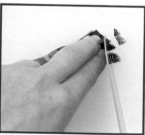

⑤ Cut off the tip of tail diagonally. This is to release the moisture in the tail and avoid splashing in hot oil.

⑥ Remove the part under 'chin'.

⑦ Remove shell carefully not to tear off flesh, but quickly.

⑧ Leave the last shell of joint still attached. This is to let the tail stand when fried.

⑨ Remove legs.

⑩ Make a few incisions along belly to avoid curling when fried.

⑪ Gently stroke, stretching the body.

⑫ Prepared prawn.

Sillago

① Using tip of knife, scrape off scales. Do not damage the skin as it has a soft fragile flesh.

② Work from both sides, cut off head.

③ Using tip of knife, pull out entrails.

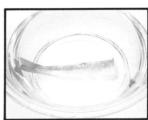

④ Wash in lightly salted iced water, pat dry.

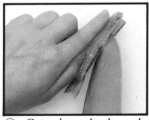

⑤ Cut along back and open flat (belly side still attached).

⑥ Work knife along backbone and remove it keeping tail attached.

⑦ Carefully slice off small bones along belly, on both sides.

⑧ Now sillago is ready for *tempura*. Frozen fish can also be used.

Squid

① Using fingers, separate the joint of body and tentacles.

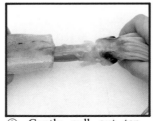

② Gently pull out tentacles. Do not break entrails.

③ Tear off triangular 'hat'.

④ Make an incision to the back and open flat.

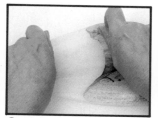

⑤ Rub the 'top' with a cloth and catch the skin. Peel gently.

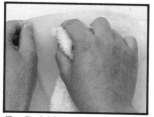

⑥ Rubbing with a wet cloth, peel the thin film. Peel the skin of 'hat' too.

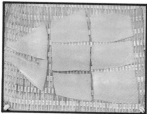

⑦ Cut into bite-size strips.

⑧ For easy biting, make a few incisions (2 incisions on one side, 1 on the other side).

Eggplant

① Wash and pat dry. Trim off the end.

② Cut in half lengthwise.

③ Cut crosswise (now quartered).

④ Make incisions in diamond pattern on skin.

Shishito Peppers

① Wash and pat dry. Remove stem end of each green pepper.

② Pierce at a few points with a skewer to avoid oil-splattering when fried.

Green Shiso Leaves

Soak in water 2–3 minutes; pat dry.

2 Make *tentsuyu* (*tempura* dipping sauce).

① Bring water to a boil and add dried bonito flakes; lower the heat. Simmer 2–3 minutes. Remove from heat.

② Set aside until bonito flakes settle, about 2 minutes. Strain.

③ Heat *mirin* in a saucepan to a boil to release alcohol.

④ Add soy sauce, *dashi* stock (process 2) and bring to a boil. Remove from heat and allow to cool. Do not refrigerate.

TEMPURA

3 Prepare condiments.

Daikon Oroshi

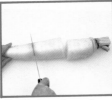    

① Wash and pat dry. Cut off 1 in (2.5 cm) from stem end and cut the remainder into 2 or 3 pieces.

② Peel the skin.

③ Grate on a grater. If using food processor, cut into chunks and turn on at medium speed.

④ When the radish becomes too small to grate, scrape off grated radish from 'teeth' with the remaining.

⑤ Place onto a bamboo mat or a strainer and allow to drain.

Momiji Oroshi

 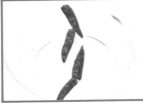 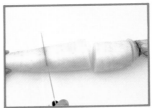 

① Wash 3–4 hot red peppers. Remove the stems and seeds.

② If the peppers are very dry, soak in water with 1–2 drops of vinegar until softened.

③ Wash *daikon* radish and pat dry. Cut off 1 in (2.5 cm) from the stem end and cut the remainder into 2 or 3.

④ Peel the skin.

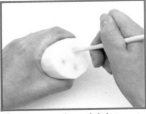   

⑤ Thrust a chopstick into cut side and make holes for each pepper.

⑥ Insert chopstick into seeded pepper and plug into the hole.

⑦ Using a fine grater, grate the pepper side. Work slowly and carefully to make finer flakes of pepper.

⑧ Place onto a bamboo mat or a strainer, and allow to drain.

Grated Ginger

① Peel thinly using a paring knife.

② To remove the skin in dents, scrape with a tip of chopstick.

③ Lay a sheet of plastic wrap on a grater, and grate ginger against the grain.

④ Gather grated ginger with plastic wrap and squeeze out excess moisture lightly. Plastic wrap is useful for grating.

To Arrange

In a small condiment server or a plate, place *daikon oroshi*, *momiji oroshi* and grated ginger.

How To Serve Tasty *Tempura*

Tempura is best served piping hot. There are a few points to make a successful *tempura*. First, select ingredients according to personal preference and recipe instructions. For deep-frying, start with light-flavored fish such as prawn or sillago, and end with rich or strong-flavored ingredients such as conger eel or *shiso* leaves. The final point is the variation of *tempura* dipping sauce (*tentsuyu*) with condiments. Sprinkling a pinch of salt to deep-fried prawns brings out the subtle sweetness of the prawns.

4 Prepare batter.

① Sift flour 2–3 times.

② In a medium bowl, add egg yolk. Stir but do not whisk.

③ Pour in iced water and mix.

④ Add sifted flour just until blended.

⑤ Using large chopsticks, mix gently so as not to make the batter glutenous. Batter will be slightly lumpy.

Seven Points In How To Make *Tempura* Batter

① Refrigerate flour and eggs. Use iced water. This is to expand the temperature difference between oil and batter.
② Sift flour so as not to make glutenous batter.
③ Combine batter ingredients only after the oil is hot enough.
④ Batter will become glutenous as time goes. So prepare only enough per portion.
⑤ When mixing flour and water, add flour into egg and water mixture.
⑥ Use thick chopsticks or fork when stirring the batter, criss-cross motion in the mixture. Never use eggbeater.
⑦ Place the bowl of batter far from the frying pan as the heat damages the quality of batter.

5 Have oil ready for frying.

① Add oil in a pan, then turn on the heat. Ideal amount of oil is 80% full in the pan. When oil becomes hot, stir for the even temperature on the bottom and the surface.

② Drop batter to test the temperature; if it floats near the surface of the oil after descending halfway to the bottom, it is ready.

How To Judge Oil Temperature Without Thermometer

Oil temperature must be controlled depending on ingredient. To tell the temperature, drop batter into oil. It reaches the bottom of pan because of its weight. To see when it's ready, watch when it floats to the surface. You can tell the temperature by the time it takes to float.

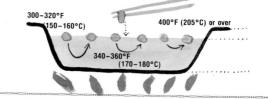

300–320°F (150–160°C)
340–360°F (170–180°C)
400°F (205°C) or over

TEMPURA

6 Start deep-frying.

 Prawn

① Pat dry. Dust with flour just before frying.

② Check the oil temperature. When it reaches 360°F (180°C), dip prawn in batter. Holding the tail, drip off excess (do not coat the tail).

③ Pinch the tail and slide into oil from the side of pan. Be careful not to splash oil.

④ Hold the tail 2–3 seconds to retain the shape; release.

⑤ Turn occasionally until golden. When the splattering bubbles are very small, it is cooked.

⑥ Drain excess oil on wire rack. Do not overlap, show side up when serving to keep crisp.

Prawns

Prawns are a must in *tempura* dishes and are universally loved by everyone. The red color, 'sweet' taste and crisp texture are irreplaceable by any other fish. They are also regarded as a 'happy food' and are always served on celebrating occasions in Japan. The Japanese name for prawn or shrimp, *ebi*, comes from an old Chinese saying which means 'A loving couple gets older together when in life, and sleep together in the same hole when they die.'

 Sillago

① When oil temperature reaches 360°F (180°C), lightly dust with flour. Pinch the tail and dip both sides in batter.

② Pull up and slide into oil. Always put serving side up as the moment battered ingredients are put into oil, the shape solidifies.

③ Turn 2–3 times in oil. This fish cooks in a short time.

④ Lift straight out from oil and drain. Do not overlap deep-fried fish.

 Squid

① Pat dry carefully as squid has a lot of moisture that splatters oil. Dust with flour and coat with batter. Deep-fry in 360°F (180°C) oil.

② Deep-fry over high heat and take it out 'Al dente'; drain.

Squid

There are numerous kinds of squid in Japan, among which calamary and common cuttlefish are most prized when cooked as *tempura*.

Fresh squid glistens in brown-black on the back and has a firm round body. Then it becomes whitish and gradually reddish brown as it loses freshness.

Preparation depends on the kind of squid, but common point is to remove the film carefully after peeling the outer skin. This film will harden and also cause oil splattering while being deep-fried. Oil splattering is also caused by wet ingredients. Thoroughly pat dry with cloth before coating.

Deep-frying

 Eggplant

① When oil temperature reaches 340°F (170°C), lightly dust with flour and dip in batter. Gently slide into oil.

② Deep-fry until heat penetrates well. Lift and drain.

Eggplant

Use the thin type for *tempura*. Fresh eggplants are spongy but firm, and dark purple in color, and with thorny tips on hard end. Avoid ones with many thorns; they have more seeds. If using thick eggplant, slice diagonally or make slits or incisions on skin side.

Shishito Peppers

① When oil temperature reaches 340°F (170°C), dip lower half of pepper in batter and gently slide into oil.

② Turning 2–3 times, deep-fry long enough to release moisture but to retain color.

③ Lift and drain.

Shishito Pepper

This is one of popular *tempura* ingredients because of its color and the miniature appearance. It is an improved variety of hot green pepper but has no hot taste. Rich in vitamins A and C. If it is not available, use green bell pepper and cut it into quarters. In either case, wash before removing hard end to prevent oil splattering.

Green *Shiso* Leaves

① When oil temperature reaches 320°F (160°C), coat only wrong side of leaf in flour, then with batter. Slide into oil coated side down.

② Deep-fry long enough to keep crispness. Lift carefully so as not to separate the leaf and coating; drain.

Green *Shiso* Leaf

Minty aromatic herb in red and green often homegrown in Japan, has fragranced aroma that enhances any accompanying food such as meats, fish, and *sushi*, and it is also used as a garnish or condiment the same way as parsley. Green *shiso* leaf is rich in iron, carotin, calcium and vitamins.
The key to good *tempura* is to let the leaves contain moisture. Soak in cold water 2-3 minutes, pat dry and coat in batter; which seals the leaf preventing 'shrinkage or weeping'.

7 Lay the table.

Give each diner an individual place setting…China plates, lacquer tray, bamboo baskets, or whatever you choose.
Line the plates with Japanese paper or paper towel, folding each to adjust the size and shape.
Arrange drained *tempura* attractively to please your eyes. For example, arrange green *shiso* leaves to let the colors of fish or prawn stand out. Or display neatly rather a large sized plate so that extra space will show the food off to advantage. If using one large plate, do not overlap *tempura*.
Provide individual sauce dishes and pour lukewarm *tentsuyu* (*tempura* dipping sauce) into individual bowls.

This is how to serve *tempura*. See "How To Eat" on page 40.

TEMPURA

Choose light-flavored seafood and vegetables with mild flavor. Make thicker batter as directed on page 54 (*kakiage*).

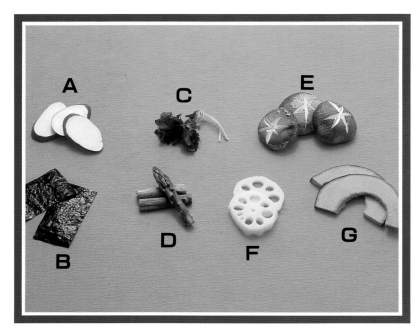

◀ **Just-fried *Tempura*** ▶

A Sweet Potatoes

 Preparation

Wash unpeeled sweet potatoes and pat dry. Cut diagonally into ¼ in (0.7 cm) slices.

To Deep-fry

Dust with flour, dip in batter. Deep-fry until soft inside, in 320°F (160°C) oil.

B *Nori* Seaweed

Preparation

Cut into bite-size pieces.

To Deep-fry

Coat only one side with batter. Carefully deep-fry in 320°F (160°C) oil.

C Trefoil

Preparation

① On a cutting board, place 2–3 stalks. Rub and roll to soften.

② Tie loosely as shown. Do not break the stalks.

③ Cut off the edges.

 To Deep-fry

Coat only stalk part with batter. Deep-fry carefully so as not to loose the color, in 320°F (160°C) oil.

D Green Asparagus

 Preparation

① Remove tough skin with a paring knife.

② Break off tough ends as far down as stalks snap easily. Cut into 2 in (5 cm) pieces.

③ Make a deep criss-cross incisions into cut ends for even cooking.

 To Deep-fry

Dust with flour and dip in batter. Deep-fry in 340°F (170°C) oil.

E *Shiitake* Mushrooms

 Preparation

① Look for even sized with thick caps. Remove stems.

② Remove dust from underside. Wash only dirty ones. Pat dry.

③ Make decorative incisions slanting the knife.

 To Deep-fry

Coat underside with batter and deep-fry until well-cooked in 340°F (170°C) oil.

F Lotus Root

 Preparation

① Peel lengthwise.

② Slice into ¼ in (0.7 cm) thickness.

③ Soak in vinegared water to prevent discoloring.

To Deep-fry

Pat dry, dust with flour, and coat with batter. Deep-fry in 340°F (170°C) oil.

G Pumpkin

 Preparation

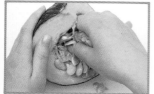

① Wash thoroughly. Remove seeds and membrane.

② Pat dry and slice into ¼ in (0.7 cm) thick wedges.

To Deep-fry

Dust with flour, coat with batter and deep-fry in 340°F (170°C) oil.

A tasty one-dish meal with hot cooked rice. *Tempura* are dipped into sauce and placed on rice. Top with prawn, squid, vegetable *tempura* or any of your choice.

INGREDIENTS: 4 servings

6 cups hot cooked rice (See p 74)
8 prawn *tempura* (See p 41)
4 squid *tempura* (See p 41)
8 *shishito* pepper *tempura* (See p 41)

Tendon Sauce
- ½ cup *dashi* stock (See p 76)
- 2 T *mirin*
- 1 T soy sauce
- ½ T sugar

* Just-fried *tempura* are best, but left-over *tempura* may be used. If using cold *tempura*, blanch in heated sauce long enough to penetrate the heat.

1 Make *tendon* sauce.

In a saucepan, bring *dashi* stock, *mirin*, soy sauce and sugar to a boil.

2 Serve.

Place hot cooked rice in serving bowl. Dip *tempura* into heated sauce and place on top of rice.

HEALTHY *TEMPURA*

As the crispness is the most important facter in this dish, only use just-fried *tempura*.

INGREDIENTS: 4 servings

10½ oz (300g) dried buckwheat
  noodles
4 prawn *tempura* (See p 41)
4 squid *tempura* (See p 41)
Soup
⎰ 5½ cups water
⎱ 4 in (10cm) square *kombu* kelp
⎱ 1 cup dried bonito flakes
⎱ ⅓ cup soy sauce
⎱ 2 T *mirin*
⎰ 1 T sugar
12–16 stalks trefoil
Seven spice powder or chili
  pepper

1 First make the soup.

① In a saucepan add water and cleaned *kombu* kelp. Cook over medium heat.

② Just before boiling point, take kelp out.

③ Add dried bonito flakes. Remove from heat just before boiling point.

④ Skim off residue and let stand until bonito flakes settle; strain.

⑤ Heat *dashi* stock, soy sauce, *mirin* and sugar to a boil.

2 Now cook noodles.

In rapidly boiling water in a deep pot, add buckwheat noodles. Occasionally stir to separate strands and cook just until tender 10–15 minutes, adding a cup of cold water if necessary. Remove from heat after boiling; drain in a colander (See p 53).

3 Serve.

① Place cooked buckwheat noodles in serving bowl. Top with *tempura*. Pour over the soup from sides of the bowl.

② Garnish with trefoil cut into 1½ in (4cm). Accompany with seven spice powder, if desired.

51

TEMPURA

Tempura and seasoned onion are bound together with egg and placed on top of hot noodle in tasty soup. This substantial dish is a favorite with everyone. Eggs must be fluffy and partly cooked.

INGREDIENTS: 4 servings

10½ oz (300 g) dried thick noodles
4 prawn *tempura* (See p 41)
1 medium onion

A {
1 cup *dashi* stock (See p 76)
4 T soy sauce
3 T sugar
1 T sake
1 t *mirin*
}

4 eggs
10 stalks trefoil

Soup

{
5 cups water
1   4 in (10cm) square *kombu* kelp
¾ cup dried bonito flakes
½ cup soy sauce
2 T *mirin*
1 T sugar
}

1 Make the soup first.

① In a large saucepan add water and cleaned *kombu* kelp (wipe with dry cloth), turn on heat to medium.

② Take out *kombu* kelp just before boiling point.

③ Add dried bonito flakes and remove from heat just before boiling point.

④ Skim off residue and allow to stand until bonito flakes settle; drain.

⑤ In a large saucepan add *dashi* stock (process 4), soy sauce, *mirin* and sugar. Bring to a boil.

THICK NOODLES WITH *TEMPURA* AND EGG

2 Then cook onion.

① Cut off core end of onion.

② Cut in half and peel.

③ Slice thinly.

④ In a medium size saucepan combine **A** ingredients and add onion. Turn on heat to medium.

⑤ When bubbly, reduce heat. Occasionally shaking pan to avoid burning, cook until onion is tender.

3 Prepare thick noodles.

① Cook noodles 10–15 minutes in abundant boiling water. (See right column)

② Drain in a colander, and place in individual serving bowls.

Japanese Noodles
Noodle dishes are one of the most popular foods in Japan. There are 'noodle stands' on the corner of the street, and even at the train station. The soups of *Kanto* (western Japan) differ to those of *Kansai* (eastern Japan). People in west of Japan like opaque-colored soups while people in east prefer soups of soy sauce varieties. Nowadays various kinds of dried noodles are available abroad. Directions are usually printed on the package: Cook in plenty of boiling water as you do for spaghetti. Heat to rapid boiling point and pour 1-2 cups water. Cooking time depends on the type of noodles, but generally cook it for 10–15 minutes over high heat. When thoroughly cooked, drain and transfer into a bowl of cold water and rinse to remove starch and gluten. Drain in colander.

4 Now make topping.

① Beat one egg each serving.

② In a small skillet, bring ¼ amount of soup and cooked onion to a boil over medium heat. When bubbly, add one portion of *tempura* and cook lightly.

③ Pour in beaten egg.

④ Cut trefoil into 1½ in (4cm) and sprinkle over; cover and remove from pan. Uncover when the egg is partly cooked.

5 Serve.

① Carefully slide hot topping onto noodles.

② Pour soup over from the sides of the bowl.

TEMPURA

Kakiage is one form of *tempura*, a mixture of vegetables and seafood is deep-fried in *tempura* batter. All ingredients are cut into same small size. Batter should be thicker than usual. Follow the instructions below.

3 oz (85g) shelled shrimp
2/3 oz (20g) burdock root
2/3 oz (20g) carrot
1/2 bunch trefoil
2 green onions
Flour for dusting

Batter
- 1 egg
- 1 1/4 cups flour
- 2/3 cup iced water

Oil for frying (to fill 80% of pan)

Tentsuyu (*tempura* dipping sauce)
- 2/3 cup water
- 1/5 cup each dried bonito flakes, *mirin*, soy sauce

Condiment
Daikon Oroshi (grated *daikon* radish)

* Parsley may be substituted for trefoil.

1 Prepare ingredients.

 Shelled Shrimp

① Clean shrimp and pat dry.

② Lightly dust with flour.

> **Seafood In *Kakiage***
>
> Enjoy variations of *kakiage*. Small shrimp may be substituted. Slices of prawn or chopped scallops for a more exciting dish. When choosing scallops, look for yellow-white firm ones.
>
> For a change, use lean ham, sausage or seasonal mushrooms, since 'kakiage' literally means 'bits of vegetables gathered and deep-fried'. It is also good with wheat flour. Try your own *kakiage*!

 Burdock Root

① Wash and scrape off skin using back of knife.

② Cut into shavings, as you do sharpening your pencil, rolling burdock with left fingers.

③ Soak in cold water to remove harsh taste.

 Carrot

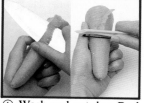

① Wash and pat dry. Peel with a peeler.

② Cut into 2 in (5 cm) julienne strips.

 Trefoil (Substitute with parsley)

① Wash and pat dry. Remove root ends.

② Cut into 2 in (5 cm) length.

 Green Onions

① Wash and pat dry. Remove root ends and withered leaves.

② Cut into 2 in (5 cm) length.

 All ingredients are assembled for deep-frying

TEMPURA

2 Make *tentsuyu* (*tempura* dipping sauce).

① Heat ⅔ cup water to a boil. Add dried bonito flakes, simmer 2–3 minutes. Remove from heat.

② Let stand until bonito flakes settle 2 minutes; strain through a fine cloth.

③ Bring *mirin* to a boil to release alcohol.

④ Add soy sauce and *dashi* stock (process 2) and bring to a boil; remove from heat. Cool to room temperature and pour into individual dish.

3 Prepare condiments.

Daikon Oroshi

① Wash *daikon* radish, pat dry. Cut off 1 in (2.5cm) from stem end. Cut the remainder into 2–3.

② Peel with a peeler.

③ Grate on a grater.

④ When radish is too small to grate, scrape off grated radish between the 'teeth'.

⑤ Drain on a bamboo mat or a colander.

4 Now make batter.

① Sift flour 2–3 times to let the air in.

② In a medium bowl add egg and stir. Do not whisk.

③ Pour ice water and stir well.

④ Add sifted flour and mix well with chopsticks until rather sticky.

5 Have oil ready for deep-frying.

① Turn on heat after pouring oil into the pan. Fill 80% of the pan. When the surface of oil looks warmed, stir gently for even temperature.

② Test the temperature by dropping a bit of batter. It is ready when the batter splashes near the surface of oil immediately after reaching near the bottom of pan. A cooking thermometer is useful.

Oil For Deep-frying

For *tempura*, animal fats are not appropriate since they are too strong in flavor and become solid in room temperature. Most suitable for *tempura* are vegetable oils. *Tempura* oil is extracted from soy beans or seed oil and has a fragrance. However quality vegetable oil is sometimes used for *tempura* as it makes a crisper and lighter flavored dish.

6 Start deep-frying.

① Add all ingredients to the batter and mix well.

② When the oil temperature reaches 330–340°F (165–170°C), scoop ¼ of batter-coated ingredients and slide into oil using chopsticks.

③ Spread evenly. Cook until half-done.

④ Turn and cook until about 20% is done, removing the splashed batter constantly.

⑤ Turn again and cook until done or crisp. Lift with chopsticks and drain well. Serve with *daikon oroshi*.

Serve immediately after deep-frying, and enjoy the crispness and flavor.

Set individual sauce dish, chopsticks and chopstick rests on the table. Serve piping hot *kakiage* and let everyone help themselves and dip into individual *tentsuyu* sauce. Add *daikon oroshi* to sauce, if desired.

Variations
(Ingredients make 4 servings)

Listed below are hints of *kakiage* combinations. Try your own ideas as well.

★ **Small dried shrimp/onion/green bell pepper:** Sprinkle *sake* over ⅔ oz (20g) small dried shrimp. Slice half onion thinly. Seed 1 green bell pepper and cut into shreds.

★ **Frozen mixed vegetables/wieners:** In a pan add frozen vegetables and heat to remove moisture. Slice 2 wieners thin.

★ *Natto* **(fermented soybeans)/green onions:** Mix 2 packets (2½–3½ oz/70–100g) *natto* and chopped scallions of the same amount. For more flavor, add more chives or scallions. Soak chopped chives in cold water before using.

★ **Ham/green onion/carrot/fresh ginger:** Chop ⅓ stalk green onion. Cut ¼ carrot into ⅜ in (1cm) cubes. Shred small piece of fresh ginger.

★ **Scallops/onion/trefoil:** Chop scallops and lightly sprinkle salt; pat dry. Slice half onion thin. Cut ½ bunch trefoil or watercress into pieces.

★ **Squid tentacles/potato/green bell pepper:** Chop squid tentacles (2 portions) and pat dry. Dust with flour. Cut 1 potato into ⅜ in (1cm) cubes and parboil. Cut 1 green bell pepper into same sized squares.

TEPPAN-YAKI

Teppan-yaki is another popular dish cooked at the table *teppan* using a thick iron plate that functions powerfully to cook meat, seafood, or vegetables. *Teppan-yaki* needs no specific ingredients except for soy sauce or other sauce ingredients. This is why *teppan-yaki* has become "A Westerners' favorite dish". Entertain your family, party or unexpected guests with this attractive free style barbecue.

Prepare table and ingredients then indulge yourselves around the *teppan*!

1 Place all ingredients and items together with the *teppan*.

Recently electric griddles are often used for *teppan-yaki*; as they are thermostatial controlled 180–400°F (80–205°C), and make an ideal utensil. If using a brand new iron plate, heat well and rub oil over the surface several times.

Arrange prepared meat (See p 61), seafood (See p 61), vegetables (See p 62) 4 sauces (See p 63) and 2 condiments (See p 63) near you. Also place individual serving dishes, chopsticks and a turner.

2 Let's take sauces and condiments!

Let everyone take their favorite sauces and condiments.
Plum Sauce: fresh and sour taste
Ketchup Sauce: good for meats and vegetables
Hot Bean Sauce: hot and sour taste
Spicy Soy Sauce: rich and pungent taste

3 Time for everyone to cook and eat.

① Heat iron plate well. Coat oil thinly. If using electric griddle, adjust the temperature, and coat with oil, if necessary. Let everyone help themselves.

② Take what is cooked and dip in sauce with condiments. Be careful of scorching while cooking.

INGREDIENTS: 4 servings

11 oz (315g) beef loin roast or round
8 clams
8 prawns
4 small eggplants
7 oz (200g) pumpkin
4 green bell peppers
4 red bell peppers
1 ear of corn
Oil for coating
Salt & pepper
Sauces
Plum Sauce
{ 4 pickled plums
{ ½ cup *dashi* stock (See p 76)
{ 1 T *mirin*
{ 1 t soy sauce
{ 1 t sesame sauce
Ketchup Sauce
{ ½ cup tomato ketchup
{ ¼ cup worcestershire sauce

Hot Bean Sauce
{ ½ T hot bean paste
{ 4 T vinegar
{ 1 T *dashi* stock (See p 76)
{ 1 t sugar
{ 1 t soy sauce
{ 1 t sesame sauce
Spicy Soy Sauce
{ 4 T soy sauce
{ 2 T red wine
{ 1 T honey
{ 1 T oyster sauce
{ 2 t grated ginger
{ 1 t crushed garlic
{ Dash of pepper
Condiments
Daikon Oroshi (grated *daikon* radish)
Chopped Chives

* Combine your favorite ingredients. Suggestions are: onion, carrot, tomato, potato, mushroom, clam, squid, ham, sausage, chicken, livers.
* Either prawn with heads on, or headless shrimp can be used. Remove legs and shell in preparation.
* A refreshing change: Serve Boston lettuce or red leaf lettuce and let everyone wrap or roll the cooked meat and vegetables.

1 Prepare the meat.

 ### If using pre-sliced meat

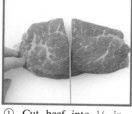 

① Cut beef into ¼ in (0.7cm) thick, about 2 in (5cm) long pieces.

② Sprinkle both sides with salt and pepper.

 ### If using frozen cut

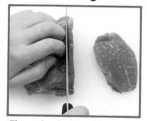

Thaw slowly in refrigerator. Slice into ¼ in (0.7cm) and sprinkle both sides with salt and pepper.

To Arrange

Line a plate with beef slices, in one layer.

2 Prepare the seafood.

 ### Clams

Cover with salted water to remove sand.

Prawn

① Wash and pat dry. Holding at the end of head and body, pull off the head. Devein.

② Cut off tail end. This is to prevent oil splattering when grilling since the pointing tail holds a drop of water.

③ Remove legs.

 ### Presentation

Place on a dish after drying well with a cloth.

TEPPAN-YAKI

3 Prepare the vegetables.

 Eggplants

① Wash and cut off end.
② Cut lengthwise in half.
③ Make incisions at ¼ in (0.7 cm) intervals.
④ Place in water to remove harshness.
⑤ Pat dry.

 Pumpkin

① Wash skin carefully, and remove seeds and membrane.
② Cut into ¼ in (0.7 cm) thick wedges. Handle cautiously not to cut your fingers.

Pumpkin
There are several kinds of pumpkins: Western pumpkins including winter squash, marrow, Japanese pumpkins which are rather small in size and dark in color, and miniature or giant pumpkins for ornamental use.
Pumpkin contains a lot of carotin and also vitamins B1, B2 and C. Look for a heavy one with firm flesh. A versatile vegetable with a great versatility, simmering, frying, steaming, stir-frying, other than mushing into soups and pies.

 Bell Peppers

① Cut off stem ends and split. If large, cut into quarters.
② Remove seeds.

 To Arrange

 Corn

① Remove skin and membrane.
② Cut into 1½ in (4 cm) pieces. Parboiling will make the cooking easier.

After pat drying, arrange eggplants, pumpkin, bell peppers and corn attractively.

4 Now make sauces.

 Plum Sauce

① Remove seeds and chop finely.

② Mix well with remaining ingredients.

 Ketchup Sauce

Mix tomato ketchup and Worcestershire sauce.

 Hot Bean Sauce

Mix all ingredients.

 Spiced Soy Sauce

Mix all ingredients.

 To Arrange

Transfer each into deep dish and provide each with spoon for serving.

5 Prepare the condiments.

 Daikon Oroshi

① Wash and cut off 1 in (2.5 cm) from stem end. Cut remainder into 2–3.

② Peel with a peeler.

③ Grate on a grater.

④ When radish is too small to grate, scrape off grated radish between the 'teeth' with the remainder.

⑤ Transfer onto a bamboo mat or a colander; drain.

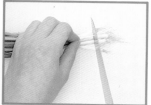 Chopped Chives

① Lightly wash and pat dry. Discard roots and withered leaves.

② Holding 7–8 stalks together, slice very thinly.

 To Arrange

Place each condiment in heap.

Following the preparation (P. 60), begin cooking and eating.

TEPPAN-YAKI

Here are several ideas to impress your guests. With additional preparation, the table looks truly unique. "Easy and tasty."

A Hawaiian Rolls

INGREDIENTS: 4 rolls
4 small frankfurters
1 slice canned pineapple
4 strips bacon

① Make a deep slash lengthwise.

② Chop pineapple and stuff into frankfurters.

③ Roll with bacon, placing ends under.

B Grilled Rice Balls

INGREDIENTS: 4 small balls
1 cup cooked rice (See p 74)
1 t green laver (*aonori*)
½ t each white and black sesame seeds
Soy sauce for coating

① Using fingers, shape cooked rice into your favorite form.

② Mix green laver and white and black sesame seeds and sprinkle over.

C Three-colored *Nori*-seaweed Rolls

INGREDIENTS: 4 rolls
4 oz (115g) processed cheese
½ block *kamaboko* (steamed fish paste)
1 small cucumber
1 sheet *nori* seaweed
Salt & pepper

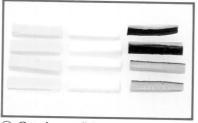

① Cut cheese, fish paste, cucumber into 2 in (5cm) long, ⅜ in (1cm) thickness.

② Sprinkle cucumber with salt and pepper.

③ Cut *nori* seaweed into 2 in (5cm) width and into same length as the ingredients (process 1).

④ With a sheet of *nori* seaweed, roll 1 stick each cheese, fish paste and cucumber.

⑤ Cut each roll into 3.

D Beef Rolls

INGREDIENTS: 4 rolls
4 thinly sliced beef
4 slices of honey roast ham
8 stalks chives
Salt & pepper

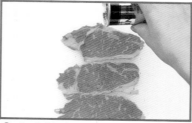

① Sprinkle beef with salt and pepper.

② Wash chives briefly and pat dry. Remove roots and withered leaves.

③ Cut chives into same length as ham.

④ Roll 3–4 stalks of chives with ham.

⑤ Roll again with beef, place ends under.

TERIYAKI STEAK

TERIYAKI STEAK   Serve sizzling hot !

The word *teriyaki* means, literally, 'a shiny broil'. Fish or meat is broiled after being marinated in soy based sauce or basted in the sauce. The 'shine' is created by soy sauce and *mirin* which gives a superb flavor. The meat will be tenderized by the marinade.

Enjoy the real *teriyaki* yourself. Tip: Serve very hot.

Shall we eat in Western manner?

Arrange the table with napkins, knives and forks. Place salad plate on the upper left, wine glass on the upper right. Check if everything is ready, and then cook the meat and serve immediately.

Sprinkle with lemon juice or dip into *daikon oroshi* (grated *daikon* radish — See p 70), if desired. Make some slashes on the meat to see the doneness.

◀ A la carte ▶

Shall we eat in Japanese manner?

Arrange the table with chopsticks and chopstick rests. Place salad plate on the upper left, wine glass on the upper right. Cook the meat and cut into bite-size pieces and arrange on a plate; serve hot.

◀ How to 'cut & serve' *teriyaki* steak ▶

① Cut broiled steak into ³/₈ in (1 cm) strips.

② Carefully place on serving plate so as not to spoil the original shape.

TERIYAKI STEAK   Ingredients/Preparation

| INGREDIENTS: 4 servings |

4 5–7 oz (140–200g) steak
Teriyaki Sauce
⎰ ⅓ cup soy sauce
⎜ 2 T *sake*
⎜ 2 T sugar
⎬ 1 T *mirin*
⎜ ½ T grated fresh ginger
⎱ Crushed garlic
2 cloves garlic
4 T vegetable oil
⅓ stalk *daikon* radish
½ lemon
Watercress for garnish

* Salad as an accompaniment: Cook fresh asparagus in salted boiling water; blanch in cold water to retain color. Cut into bite-size pieces. Wash cherry tomatoes and pat dry. Arrange on individual plate and serve with mayonnaise sauce, salt or dressing of your choice.

1 Prepare the meat first.

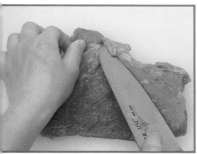

① Trim away excess fat and tough fibers.

② Using back of knife or a mallet, tenderize the meat.

③ Combine sauce ingredients.

④ Marinate beef in *teriyaki* sauce.

⑤ Let stand 30 minutes, then turn the meat over and allow another 30 minutes.

How To Choose Meat For *Teriyaki*

Teriyaki does not require very high-quality beef such as tenderloin or Sirloin. Rather tough meat such as round or chuck steak will be tenderized by the marinade and will create flavor. This is one of the reasons that this dish has gained world recognition.

TERIYAKI STEAK **Grilling**

2 Make *daikon oroshi* (grated *daikon* radish).

① Trim stem end and cut into 2 or 3.

② Peel with a peeler.

③ Grate on a grater.

④ Scrape off grated radish between 'teeth' also.

⑤ Transfer onto a bamboo mat or a colander, drain lightly.

3 Prepare lemon wedges.

① Wash lemon briefly and pat dry. Trim off ends.

② Cut lengthwise, and then into even wedges.

4 Now cook the meat.

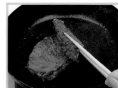

① Remove skin of garlic.

② Slice thinly. Divide into 4.

③ Heat 1 T oil in a skillet, cook and stir one portion of garlic over low heat.

④ Take out lightly browned garlic; the aroma is released. Set aside.

⑤ Broil each steak over medium heat. Watch carefully since marinated meat scorches easily. Turn over and cook.

5 Serve it.

① On a large plate (10 in, 25cm diam), arrange cooked meat.

② Place crisp-fried garlic slices on top.

③ Garnish with *daikon oroshi*, lemon wedges and watercress.

Let's eat following the directions on page 68!

Chicken is marinated in soy sauce and *mirin*, and then broiled to 'give' a rich flavor and color. The chicken and marinade sauce compliment each other. Serve cold also!

4 chicken thighs (18 oz/500 g)
***Teriyaki* Sauce**
- ⅕ cup soy sauce
- 1 T sake
- 1 T sugar
- 1 t mirin
- 1 t grated fresh ginger

Vegetable oil
Red pickled ginger for a garnish
Sansho powder (Japanese pepper) optional

1 Prepare the chicken.

① Using a fork, prick the skin side for effective cooking.

② Combine all sauce ingredients and marinate chicken approx 20 minutes, turn over and allow another 20 minutes. Then broil.

2 Grill it.

① Heat 1 T oil in a skillet, and place chicken skin side down. Cook over medium heat until golden brown.

② Turn over and covered with lid and cook over very low heat 5–6 minutes.

3 Serve it.

③ Take out chicken and discard fat from the skillet. Then pour 2 T marinade sauce per portion.

④ Bring to a boil and add chicken. Cook and stir over low heat to glaze.

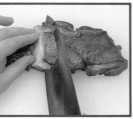

① Cut the chicken carefully as shown.

② Arrange on a plate and garnish with red pickled ginger. Sprinkle with *sansho* powder, if desired.

In this recipe the *teriyaki* sauce flavor blends well with fish. *Teriyaki* sauce is brushed on many times while being cooked to produce a rich flavor. In Japan, fish '*teriyaki*' is a favorite seafood dish.

INGREDIENTS: 4 servings

4 fillets fish (yellowtail, tuna, salmon)
8 *shishito* peppers or 4 green bell peppers
4 green *shiso* leaves

Teriyaki Sauce
- 5 T *mirin*
- 3 T soy sauce
- 1 T salad oil

* Fish may be broiled on a broiler. Preheat it well and broil the serving side first. If using skewers, thread a fillet on 2 metal skewers, forming the letter V. Cook with high heat.

1 Prepare fish.

Wash fillets briefly and pat dry.

2 Prepare vegetables.

Wash *shishito* peppers and *shiso* leaves and pat dry. To prevent 'explosion', prick *shishito* peppers.

3 Prepare *teriyaki* sauce.

① Put soy sauce and *mirin* in a saucepan, cook over low heat.

② Stirring constantly, simmer until the sauce reduces to ¹/₅ amount or until sticky.

4 Grill fish now.

① Heat oil in a skillet, add fillets serving sides down.

② Grill over medium heat until brown or almost burning. Turn over to cook the other side.

③ When both sides are brown, brush on *teriyaki* sauce and reduce heat. When the surface becomes dry, brush sauce; repeat until glazed, 2–3 times.

5 Serve it.

On individual serving plate, lay green *shiso* leaf and place *teriyaki* fillet. Briefly fry *shishito* peppers and brush on the *teriyaki* sauce; serve as a garnish.

INFORMATION

PREPARATION

Rice Cooking

There are two types of rice available; white short-grain rice and white long-grain rice. Use white short-grain rice for Japanese dishes. The short-grain rice is more glutenous than the long-grain rice. In the U.S., short-grain rice is grown extensively in California. Newly cropped rice needs less water and slightly shorter cooking time than old rice. A little practice is needed to make perfect rice, however if you cook a lot of rice, an automatic rice cooker will make your work a lot easier, so it's a good investment.

Following is a key to shiny and fluffy rice. Go ahead with these basic tips for successful rice cooking. It's easy.

1. Measure rice carefully.

2. Wash rice in a big bowl of water. Rub grains gently since wet grains break easily.

3. Remove any bran or polishing agent. Drain off water well. Repeat this step until water is almost clear.

4. To make a fluffy and moister rice, set rice aside for at least 30 minutes in summer and one hour in winter. This allows ample time for rice to absorb the water.

5. In cooking pot, add rice and correct amount of water. Cover with lid.

Rice increases in volume as it cooks, twice to three times, depending on the kind of rice you use.

COOKED RICE	RICE	WATER
2½ cups	1 cup	1¼ cups
5 cups	2 cups	2½ cups
7½ cups	3 cups	3¾ cups
10 cups	4 cups	5 cups

PREPARATION

HOW TO COOK

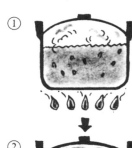 **MEDIUM HEAT UNTIL WATER BOILS**
Cook rice over medium heat until water boils. Do not bring to boiling point quickly. If the quantity of rice is large, cook rice over high heat from the beginning. The heat can be carried into the center of rice if cooked over medium heat.

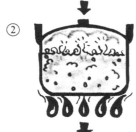 **HIGH HEAT FOR 1 MINUTE AFTER BOILING**
When it begins to boil, turn heat to high and cook for 1 minute. Never lift lid while cooking. Since the lid might bounce from the pressure of the steam, it is better to place a weight, or some dishes on the lid. Rice absorbs enough water.

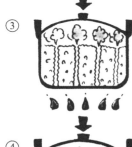 **TURN HEAT TO LOW FOR 4-5 MINUTES**
Turn heat to low and cook for 4-5 minutes (Be careful not to overboil). Then the pot begins to steam.

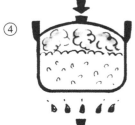 **LOWEST HEAT FOR 10 MINUTES**
Reduce heat to the lowest for 10 minutes. Every grain of rice absorbs water and becomes plump. It is liable to burn, so cook over the lowest heat.

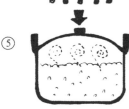 **TURN OFF AND LET STAND FOR 10 MINUTES**
Turn off the heat and let rice stand, covered for 10 minutes. During this 10 minutes the grains are allowed to "settle", and the cooking process is completed by the heat retained in the rice and the walls of the pot.

AUTOMATIC RICE COOKER

Today rice is cooked daily in many households in an automatic electric or gas rice cooker. The automatic rice cooker, an appliance developed in the postwar period, cooks perfect rice. Put washed rice in the cooker, add water. There are measurment marks in the cooker for water and rice volume. Then cover and turn on. Automatic controls take over cooking, reducing heat at exact time, and also in some models, the rice is kept warm till needed. Cookers come in various sizes, from tiny ones holding only a few cups to large ones used in restaurants. Automatic rice cookers, either electric or gas can be obtained at oriental stores.

PREPARATION

How To Make *Dashi* Stock

Good *dashi* stock is a key to all Japanese dishes. It enhances not only soups but any recipe. If you can master *dashi* stock making then you'll master the basic technique of Japanese cooking. There are two requirements for making *dashi* stock: Be quick and never boil the liquid.

Keep leftover *dashi* stock not more than 2–3 days in refrigerator, or freeze it in ice cube tray. Use as soon as possible since longer storage will loose the flavor.

Kombu kelp stock
Makes approx 4 cups

4 C	(1 qt)	water
6 in	(15cm)	length *kombu* kelp (1 1/3 oz/40g)

Wipe kelp with a damp cloth (do not wash, or much of the flavor will be lost), soak in 4 cups of water, and let it sit for an hour. Heat to boiling point, but remove the kelp just before the water actually boils.

Bonito stock
Makes approx 4 cups

4 C	(1 qt)	water
4 in	(10cm)	square *kombu* kelp (1 oz/30g)
1 C		dried bonito flakes (1/3–1/2 oz/10–15g)

A) *Ichiban-dashi* (Primary *dashi*): Put kelp in 4 cups of water. Heat, uncovered, over medium high heat until the water reaches boiling point; remove the kelp immediately. Add 1/4 cup water and heat. Add 1 cup of dried bonito flakes just before the water reaches boiling point. When the foam begins to rise, reduce heat and simmer for 10 seconds. Turn off heat, and add a pinch of salt which will keep the water from absorbing more bonito flavor and tasting too strong. Let stand until the flakes sink to the bottom. Strain and store.

B) *Niban-dashi* (Secondary *dashi*): Primary *dashi* is best for clear soups. Secondary *dashi* can be used for thick soups, cooking vegetables and many other ways as a cooking stock.
Place the kelp and bonito flakes reserved from the primary *dashi* in 4 cups water. Heat to boiling point, reduce heat and simmer for 15 minutes. Turn off heat and strain.

Sardine stock
Makes approx 4 cups

4 C	(1 qt)	water
2 T	*sake*	
10 dried small sardines		
4 in	(10cm)	square *kombu* kelp (1 oz/30g)

As dried small sardines produce a stock with a strong fish flavor, this stock is used mostly for *miso* soups. Remove heads and intestines of 10 pieces of dried sardine. This proccess reduces bitterness and strong fish flavor from stock. After washing, soak in 5 cups of water 2–3 hours. Heat until the water just reaches body temperature. Strain.

Instant *dashi*
Makes approx 4 cups

4 C	(1 qt)	water
1/3 T		instant *dashi* mix (1/8 oz/4.5g)

Add instant *dashi* mix, to boiling water and stir until powder dissolves.
Variation: Use the liquid in which dried *shiitake* mushrooms have been soaked. Add 1 teaspoon instant mix to 1 cup water and mixed with the *shiitake* liquid.

PREPARATION

How To Make *Teriyaki* Sauce

Teriyaki sauce is made of good quality soy sauce and some alcoholic seasoning such as *mirin* or *sake*. Its purpose is to tenderize the meat and at the same time to give a distinctive flavor.
Blending proportions of sauce ingredients depends on what to marinate in (See chart below). Marinate for 10–60 minutes.
To get a better glaze, heat remaining sauce in a small saucepan, until thick and sticky or until reduced to 10% in quantity, over low heat. Apply 2–3 coats over grilled food 2–3 times using a brush. It may give better flavor.

INGREDIENTS	Soy sauce	Sugar	*Mirin*	*Sake*	Crushed garlic	Grated ginger
SEAFOOD (1 lb)	¼ C	1 T	¼ C			½ T
MEAT (1 lb)	¼ C	½ t		1 T	1 clove	2 T
POULTRY (1 lb)	⅔ C	3 T	½ C	1 T	1 clove	1 T

How To Soften Dried Foods

Dried *Shiitake* Mushrooms
Rinse off dirt and cover with water for 30 minutes, cap sides up. Weight lightly to keep the mushrooms under water. In case of hurry, cover with boiling water and ½ teaspoon sugar. Reserve the soaking water and use it as *dashi* stock.

Dried Bean Threads
Another kind of gelatin noodle. This kind is easier to handle because it does not lose shape when cooked. To soften, soak in warm water until the center becomes transparent; drain.

Dried Gourd Strips (*kampyo*)
Gourd is peeled thinly into long strips and dried well. Look for a flexible one with milky white color, with sweet fragrance, and of even width.
To soften rub well in water and squeeze lightly. Sprinkle with generous amount of salt and rub well with fingers. Rinse off salt and cook briefly in boiling water. When tender, drain in a colander and allow to cool.

Dried *Wakame* Seaweed
Dried *wakame* seaweed increases its volume to 3–4 times when reconstituted. Cover with abundant water until the 'flesh' becomes thicker and flexible. Over-soaking will damage the texture. To draw out a fresh green color, blanch in boiling water and rinse in cold water at once. This method will also remove the odor.

Freeze-dried *Tofu* (*koya dofu*)
Soak in warm water (about 140°F, 60°C). Place a light lid on top to keep *tofu* under water. When completely softened, transfer into fresh water and press out opaque water several times. Squeeze out well.

Hijiki Seaweed
Look for shiny black one which is crisp dry. The volume will increase 6–7 times when reconstituted. Soak in abundant water until soft, wash thoroughly. Parboil before cooking.

Spongy Wheat Gluten Bread (*yakifu*)
Wheat gluten is mixed with starch, flour and yeast, baked lightly and dried. Look for un-dyed, uniformed shape. Generally cover with water for 10–30 minutes until the center is soft; squeeze out water lightly.

Dried Cloud Ears (*kikurage*)
Black mushrooms which grow on mulberry trees. Look for well-dried whole mushrooms. Soak in water for 10–20 minutes until widely spread. Use lukewarm water when in a hurry. Wash carefully and remove roots. They swell about 5 times after softening.

CUTTING METHODS

Basic Cutting Methods

When preparing ingredients use a sharp knife. Cut to bite size pieces making them easy to cook, and eat.

For decorative cuts, use the tip of knife. For peeling use the lower part of blade. The part from the center towards the tip is used for most cutting work.

Rounds

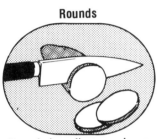

Round ingredients such as *daikon* radish or carrot are cut into the same thickness.

Diagonal Slices

Thin round ingredients such as cucumber are sliced diagonally giving a large surface.

"Paring" Thin Fillets

Soft or fragile ingredients are placed flat and pared off with the knife parallel to the cutting board.

Quarter Rounds

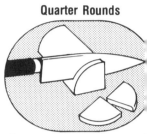

Large round ingredients such as turnip or *daikon* radish are split into quarters and then sliced.

Half-rounds

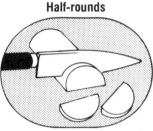

Large round ingredients such as *daikon* radish are split into halves and then sliced.

Wedges

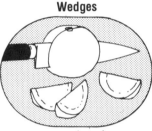

Ingredients such as lemon or onion are split into quarters or eighths.

Rolling Wedges

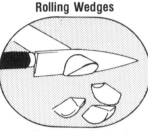

Ingredients are rolled and cut diagonally to give more sides for seasoning.

Rectangles

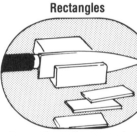

Large ingredients such as *daikon* radish are cut into 2 in (5 cm) length and then sliced into ½ in (1.5 cm) thickness.

Shreds

Ingredients are sliced into thin rectangles of 2–2½ in (5–6.5 cm) length, layered and cut into thin matchlike sticks parallel to the fibers.

Sticks

Ingredients such as potato, carrot or bamboo shoot are cut into 2–2½ in (5–6.5 cm) long, ⅜ in (1 cm) wide sticks.

Dices

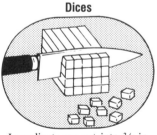

Ingredients are cut into ⅜ in (1 cm) wide sticks, and then into ⅜ in (1 cm) cubes.

Mincing

Ingredients such as ginger root or green onion are shredded and chopped finely.

Shavings

Tough ingredients such as burdock root are rolled and cut into thin shavings.

Peeling into thin sheet.

In order to make long strings, *daikon* radish or carrot is peeled in a continuous thin sheet to the center.

Flower Cut

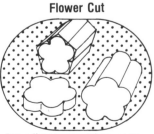

Ingredients are cut into pentagon, and then trimmed into 'plum blossom'. It is sliced and used as a decoration.

Trimming

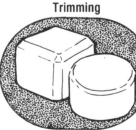

To retain the shape while being simmered, corners of ingredient are trimmed away.

COOKING TIPS

Soup Making

Soup plays an important role in a Japanese meal. No Japanese meal is perfect without one soup at least. There are basically two different kinds of soups, clear and thick. Clear soup is usually served at the beginning of a full Japanese meal. Then there is the thick soup. *Miso* soup, fermented soy bean paste soup, is a kind of thick soup. *Miso* soup may be served at the beginning of an informal meal or at the end of a full course meal. It is a must in the traditional Japanese breakfast. Thus millions of Japanese households serve different types of *miso* soup not only at breakfast but at lunch and dinner daily. Japanese clear and thick soups are based on *dashi* stock which differs completely from Western chicken or beef stock. It is based on kelp, dried bonito flakes and dried small sardines. *Dashi* stock is relatively simple to make, but like everything else in the kitchen, it demands attention to detail. See page 76 for basic *dashi* stock recipes.

Raw Fish

Fresh fish that is eaten raw as *sashimi* and *sushi* must be prepared from fish that has not been out of the water for more than 24 hours. Also it must be properly chilled, otherwise most fish has a shelf life of about five days. Of course the ideal fish is that which you catch yourself.

When buying fish for *sashimi* or *sushi* ask the fishmonger to cut the fish into slices, cubes, whatever you want.

If you are in doubt about the freshness of fish, do not eat it raw. Cook it according to personal preference or marinate it in *teriyaki* sauce and broil. Also no fresh water fish are eaten raw in *sushi* because of the possible presence of parasites. It's similar to eating pork which hasn't been cooked properly. The following are points to check for freshness.

FRESH FISH

1. Mild characteristic odor, but not too strong or "fishy".
2. Bright, full, clear eyes, not milky or sunken.
3. Bright red gills, not muddy gray, free from slime.
4. Bright characteristic sheen on scales.
5. The scales adhere tightly to body, unblemished, without any reddish patches along the ventral area.
6. Firm or rigid body when pressed with fingers.
7. Elastic, firm flesh that does not separate easily from the bones or doesn't indent when handled.
8. Freshly cut appearance with no "leathery" traces of yellowing, browning or drying visible in the flesh.
9. Sweetish and often cucumber-like odor.

FROZEN FISH

1. Should be solidly frozen, tightly wrapped with little or no air space between fish and wrapper. Should be moisture vapor-proven.
2. Should be kept at a storage temperature below −10°F (−23°C) in the retail food cabinet.
3. There should be no discoloration, fading or drying out evidence.

STORING FISH

1. Since shellfish and fish are the most perishable foods, they should be used as soon as possible.
2. Wash the fish in cold, slightly salted water. Make sure to wash the cavity well. Remove excess moisture with paper towels. Then wrap in waxed paper or freezer wrap. Keep in the refrigerator. Handle the fish as quickly as possible.
3. Frozen fish should be kept frozen solid in the freezer wrapped or in a suitable container. Do not thaw frozen fish at room temperature (before cooking), except when necessary, for ease in handling. Thawing frozen fish is best achieved at refrigerated temperature. Once the fish has been thawed out, cook it immediately. Never refreeze fish that has been thawed out. It is advisable not to keep fish frozen for more than three months.

To remove the odor from utensils, use solution of baking soda and water. (about 1 tsp. soda to a quart of water).

To get rid of "fishy" odors on the hands or the cutting board, rub with lemon juice, sliced lemon, vinegar or salt before washing and rinse well. A small amount of toothpaste rubbed on the hands and rinsed off is also a good deodorizer.

Wine, vinegar, ginger, lemon, onion, garlic, in the recipe help to minimize the odor of cooked fish.

COOKING TIPS

Grilling, Broiling, Pan-frying, Baking

Apart from eating fish raw, grilling is the best preferable method. Japan has access to a variety of fish and shellfish in the seas surrounding the country. So raw fish and seafood have always been valued and appreciated and have become an integral part of the diet. When they grill fish, it is served as if the fish on the plate is swimming in water. The grilling method is used to cook food quickly over very high heat so that the outside is crisp while the inside flesh remains tender and moist. The ingredients must be fresh. Grilling can be done in two different ways; direct and indirect heat. If you do charcoal grill, prepare charcoal fire in advance so that heat gets very hot. For stove top grilling, coat the rack with thin film of oil, then heat before you place food on. Fish and meats are often marinated or basted with marinade sauces before and during cooking. Marinade sauces are combinations of *sake, mirin* or sugar, soy sauce and fresh ginger which has the same tenderizing enzyme as papaya and pineapple. Since everything is eaten with chopsticks, food is cut into bite-size pieces except small whole fish. This also reduces both marinating and grilling time. Grill 60% on one side and 40% on the other side. For pan-frying, heat; add a small amount of oil. Heat the oil, then tilt the skillet to cover the surface. When the oil begins to form a light haze, it is ready to pan-fry the ingredients. Cook over high heat, so that fish or meat except pork is tender and moist inside and the flavor is sealed in. If longer cooking is necessary, reduce heat and cover for a few minutes. You may need to add some marinade sauce to the pan. Then remove the lid and continue to cook until all liquid evaporates. For oven baking, preheat the oven to the required temperature and place food in the center of the oven to allow for even baking. Microwave ovens are not recommended for Japanese cooking. Microwave cooking takes moisture out of fish and will not give a crispy finish. To eliminate fish odor in the kitchen after cooking, heat a small amount of soy sauce in skillet and burn. The soy sauce aroma helps to remove the fish odor.

Steaming

Steaming is one of the best way of retaining more nutrients and natural flavor than other conventional means of cooking. Steaming seals in the natural juices of meats and vegetables which are delicious when served over rice.

There are many different types of steamers available. Wok with a cover will work as a good steamer. Multitiered bamboo steamers may be purchased. However, a large pot with a cover will suffice for the purpose of steaming food.

Steaming racks are necessary to support and elevate the plate or bowl which hold food steamed in a wok. A round cake rack will do just as well as commercially available steaming racks. You may improvise, using water chestnut cans with both ends removed. The rack should be put in the center of the wok or pan.

All steamers operate according to the same basic principle. The efficient circulation of steam is of paramount importance. Bamboo steamers have several tiers in which many dishes can be steamed simultaneously. The tiers and cover are set on top of a wok containing boiling water. There are also metal steamers consisting of a pot to hold the water and usually two tiers and a cover. For example, the bottom pot cooks soup stock while the two tiers are used to steam two other separate dishes. In this manner, many dishes may be steamed at once saving time and energy.

Follow the steps below for effective steaming

1) Pour water into the wok or pot so that the water level stands one inch below the steaming rack or dish of food.
2) Cover the wok and bring the water to a full boil.
3) Use heatproof dishes only for steaming.
4) Place the dish of food atop the steaming rack. Cover and bring to the boiling point again. Turn the temperature down to medium high and allow to steam for the specified time.
5) Check the water level when longer steaming is necessary.

Deep-frying

Tempura is a representative "batter-fried" food in Japan. It is probably the best known Japanese dish.

Four points for successful *tempura*

1) Fresh ingredients
2) Good vegetable oil
3) Constant frying temperature
4) Lumpy batter

Prepare all ingredients to be deep-fried ahead of time. Preferably keep them in a refrigerator until last munite. Make the *tempura* batter just before the actual deep-frying. The *tempura* batter, mixture of ice water, eggs and flour, should never be stirred well. Mix lightly—batter should be lumpy. All food should be thoroughly dried before dredging. If you prefer a thick coating to thin batter, use less ice water than the recipe (See page 41).

In general, deep-frying requires a large amount of oil in the wok, heavy cast-iron skillet or deep-fryer. The use of polyunsaturated vegetable oil is strongly recommended for deep-frying. None of the pure vegetable oils contains cholesterol. The right temperature for deep-frying is 330–355°F (165–180°C). The oil should reach this temperature before any ingredients are added. An easy way to tell whether the oil has reached the desired temperature is by adding a drop of batter into the oil. If the drop of batter reaches the bottom and slowly returns to the surface, the oil is not yet hot enough. If the batter drops half way to the bottom and immdediately bounces up to the surface, the oil is ready for deep-frying. Drop in ingredients and deep-fry until golden. Adjust the temperature to maintain a constant frying temperature. Frying temperature of 340°F (170°C) is recommended for vegetables. Use deep-frying thermometer to maintain a constant oil temperature. Skim the surface of the oil occasionally to keep it clean. Start with vegetables and then shrimp which requires a higher temperature. The oil used for deep-frying can be saved and reused. To grant your oil longer life, remove crumbs with a fine mesh strainer. The quality of used oil is judged by its clarity, not by the number of times used nor the length of time used. Fresh oil is light in color and clear. If the used oil is still relatively clear, it is readily usable again. For the second time around, it is recommended to deep-fry chicken or meats coated with bread crumbs. To remove odor in oil, deep-fry some potatoes uncoated. The moisture in potato absorbs odor while it is deep-fried. The proportion of 3:1 (used oil: fresh oil) is also usable again for deep-frying meats and chicken, but not for *tempura*. To store the used oil, first strain with a fine mesh strainer while oil is still hot. Then place the oil in a heat-proof container and allow to cool. Cover and store in dark and cool place or in the refrigerator.

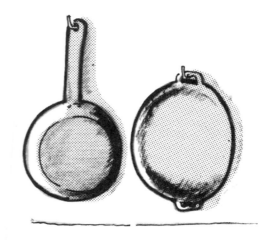

Stir-frying, Sautéing

This cooking method combines the elements of high heat and constant tossing to seal in the flavor and juices of meat and vegetables. Thus, this technique is often used for Chinese cooking. Stir-frying cooks protein foods thoroughly at the same time leaving them tender and juicy. Vegetables retain their natural color and crisp texture when stir-fried. It is important that slices are uniform in size so that they can be cooked evenly. Some vegetables may need parboiling before stir-frying. Prepare all neccessary seasonings before stir-frying. Heat the wok or skillet until it barely gets hot and add a small amount of oil (usually 2 T), then roll the oil around to cover the surface (of the wok). When the oil begins to form a light haze, add the ingredients. Follow the recipe and remember to adjust the temperature control at the proper stir-frying temperature. Actual stir-frying involves vigorous arm action in the constant stirring and tossing of the food. Serve immediately while still hot.

COOKING TIPS

Simmering

A full course Japanese meal consists of raw fish which is *sashimi*, a broiled or grilled food and a simmered food. So, simmered foods play an important role in the Japanese kitchen.

Simmering food requires special preparation

1) Simmering liquid is generally made of primary *dashi*, *ichiban-dashi* (See p 76) seasoned with *sake*, *mirin* or sugar, salt, soy sauce and/or *miso*. Sake and *mirin* are often used in Japanese cooking. They are mild in taste and add zest to the food.
2) You may need some special cutting techniques for vegetables such as diagonal slices, flower-cuts, trimming to enhance the appearance of the finished dish.
3) Some ingredients need parboiling to remove harsh or bitter taste and rawness. Also, some ingredients take longer to cook. These ingredients are sometimes pre-cooked in different pans, then added to the simmering liquid.

   Simmered food can be served as a single dish or as one-pot dish. The ingredients and simmering liquid for the one-pot dishes are prepared ahead of time and arranged attractively on large plate.

The size of the pot is determined by the amount of ingredients to be cooked. For simmering whole fish or fish fillets, use a wide flat-bottomed pan. A thick-bottomed pot will distribute the heat more evenly. If simmering for longer time, use a deep pot that holds an ample amount of simmering liquid. Slow electric cooker will have the same effect.
Indispensable for simmering is a drop lid which is a light-weight wooden lid slightly smaller than the pot. It is made of well-dried cypress or cedar. It is placed directly on top of the food to keep it immersed in the liquid, enabling the flavors to be absorbed. Wood is likely to absorb the liquid in the pot and many odors, so always soak the drop-lid in a water for a few minutes before using. Heat-proof flat plate, aluminum foil and heavy butcher-paper are good substitutes for a wooden lid. Skim off occasionally. Use light seasoning for simmering liquid. The less the better. You can always add more later. In general add sugar or *mirin* first, then salt, rice vinegar (if recipe calls for) and soy sauce. Remember to control simmering temperature so that the liquid can be slowly absorbed into the ingredients.

Nabemono Cooking (one-pot dishes)

Nabemono includes any dish that is cooked in one pot and eaten on the table. Therefore it has a great many varieties besides *sukiyaki* and *shabu-shabu*, and one of the main characteristics is in the cooking stock. In *sukiyaki* you only pick up solid ingredients from the pot, while in *yosenabe* you take the broth together and enjoy it as a soup. In *shabu-shabu, mizutaki* or *chirinabe*, you take the cooked but unseasoned ingredients and dip into sauces. In *dotenabe*, the brown broth is enjoyed as a *miso*-based soup. In *oden-nabe* fish products and vegetables are stewed for a long time and eaten with the broth.
In any type of *nabemono*, you can choose whatever ingredients you prefer. Basically *nabemono* needs no special cooking technique, but there are several points: When selecting ingredients, think not only of the colors but the affinity too. Avoid harsh-tasting or strong-odor or fragile food. When preparing, cut each ingredient according to its cooking time so that all ingredients are ready to eat at same time. Some food needs parboiling. Burdock root should be parboiled and blanched in cold water. *Daikon* radish and *konnyaku* (devil's tongue) must be parboiled to remove harsh taste. Dried foods should be softened well.

COOKING TIPS

Vegetables & Salads

Many vegetable dishes that would be served hot in Western kitchens are served at room temperature in Japan (as salads). The cooking method is to enhance nature's flavor and no matter what a vegetable dish is called for, it will be part of a meal with a main course of fish, meat, chicken and so on. Also it can be served as a single dish. Vegetables are washed often both prior to cooking and afterwards to preserve their natural colors. Cutting techniques are important and much attention is paid to little details such as assembling vegetables with other foods, raw or cooked vegetables are served with dressings which are poured over them just beforehand.

Cooking Rice

Cooked rice translated as ''*gohan*'' is eaten for breakfast, lunch, dinner, or even as a snack. Certainly nothing is more important in Japan. Japanese rice is the short-grain kind. There are 200 different varieties of rice growing in Japan. It is almost impossible to try all, but there are a few basic rules to make good cooked rice. Follow the directions on page 74 for regular rice cooking.

Noodles

There are varieties of packaged noodles readily available. Usually made from wheat flour and are sold both dried and precooked. Noodle dishes are very popular in Japan and eaten at any time. A bowl of hot steaming noodles in winter or a chilled noodle dish on a hot summer day is refreshing. Cooking noodles is similar to cooking spaghetti, unless the package has special directions.

Basic cooking methods

Fill ⅔ of a large saucepan with water and bring to a boil. Add the noodles to the boiling water, stirring with chopsticks to keep noodles separate. Bring water to a boil again; add 1 cup of water and bring back to a boil. Repeat the process 2–3 times until noodles are tender. Do not overcook. Drain the noodles in a colander and rinse under cold running water and remove gluten. Drain. They may be reheated. Put the noodles into a saucepan and pour boiling water over. Let stand for a few minutes, just long enough to heat them through. Drain and serve with dipping sauce or broth. The noodles get their flavor from the broth and the condiments. Making *dashi* stock is the first step to make good noodle dishes. See page 76 for basic *dashi* stock.

Pickling

Pickles are eaten with many dishes as a garnish to enhance both appearance and taste. There are all sorts of ways to make pickles with different ingredients. But some pickles have an aroma slightly repellent to Westerners—especially rice bran, the most common pickling medium. Pickles do not need to be so strange in taste. Since everyone is very cautious about intake of salt these days, there are many ways to preserve food without heavy salting. Using *kombu* kelp is one way. Chinese cabbage, *daikon* radish, cucumber, eggplant and califlower are commonly used for pickling.

UTENSILS

KNIVES

All-purpose knife
(Made of stainless steel)

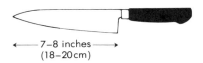

⟵ 7–8 inches ⟶
(18–20 cm)

Kitchen cleaver (*deba-bocho*)
(Made of carbon steel)
This is used for fish, meat and poultry with bones.

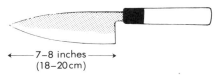

⟵ 7–8 inches ⟶
(18–20 cm)

Sashimi slicer (*tako-biki*)
(Made of carbon steel)
This is used for slicing fish fillets.

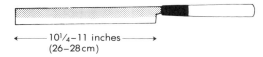

⟵ 10¼–11 inches ⟶
(26–28 cm)

Sashimi slicer (*yanagi-ba*) "Willow-leaf" slicer
(Made of carbon steel)

⟵ 10¼–11 inches ⟶
(26–28 cm)

Vegetable knife (*usuba-bocho*)
(Made of carbon steel)

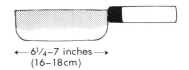

⟵ 6¼–7 inches ⟶
(16–18 cm)

Kitchen scissors
(Made of stainless steel)

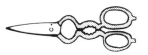

Cheese knife
(Made of carbon steel)

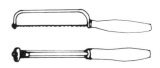

Paring knife
(Made of stainless steel)

Frozen food knife
(Made of stainless steel)

Bread knife
(Made of stainless steel)

Knife Sharpening Stone and Knife Sharpener

Knives made of carbon steel should be sharpened with a stone. Always wash in hot water and wipe dry with a cloth after use. Moisten stone with water, placing wet cloth or kitchen towel under the stone to secure it. Place the beveled cutting edge of the blade flat on the stone. Push the blade away from you to the edge of the stone. Bring back to start and repeat this stroke with some pressure for 10–20 times and 2–3 times on the other side. All purpose knife should be sharpened with same number of strokes on both sides. Keep your knives sharp.

The beveled cutting edges

correct   wrong   wrong

UTENSILS

CUTTING BOARD

The sharpness of the blade is affected by the cutting board you use. Wood gives the best surface. In Japan, cypress (*hinoki*) seen at *sushi* restaurants is one of the most common material. Willow and pine are also used as well as plastic. After using, wash quickly with warm water and wipe dry. To get rid of fishy odors on the cutting board, rub with sliced lemon, lemon juice, vinegar or salt before washing and rinse well. Do not store while still damp.

CHOPSTICKS (*HASHI*)

Come in various lengths and styles. China, Korea and Vietnam also use chopsticks and each country has different types of chopsticks. Traditional Japanese chopsticks are made of bamboo or cedar. These materials were used so that the fine surface of the pottery would not be scratched and also Japanese like the touch of wood rather than metal. Chopsticks are all-purpose handy utensils for oriental cooks. Use them to reach the bottom of deep pots, pans and bowls and to stir, beat, whisk, turn food and lift all sorts of food.

Eating chopsticks

Today Japanese chopsticks are so useful for any type of cooking that it is worth the effort to learn how to use them.

How To Use Chopsticks

1. Chopsticks are placed on the chopstick rest thinner ends on your left. Hold the center with your right fingers.	2. Pick up and add left fingers beneath. Immediately slide your right fingers towards right ends.	3. Now hold steadily, the upper stick between thumb and forefinger, the lower stick between the tip of third finger and the base of thumb, with middle finger lifting the upper stick.	4. Release left fingers. Fix the lower stick and move the upper stick up and down using forefinger and middle finger.

Cooking chopsticks

They are longer than ordinary eating chopsticks, 12 in (30cm) or longer. Choose the proper length for comfort and ease of handling best suited to you. If you can't find the proper length of chopsticks, simply go out and cut yourself some long and straight twigs and make your own. Pointed chopsticks are the best. You may need to reshape the point by using a sharp knife. Wet the chopsticks before using so that the cooking juice will not be absorbed into the chopsticks. Usually they are joined at the top by a piece of string used to hang them when not in use.

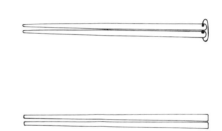

Serving chopsticks

These are almost twice as long as eating chopsticks, made of natural wood and with pointed tips.

UTENSILS

Cast-iron Pans

The most adequate pan for *sukiyaki* is cast-iron which conducts heat quickly and maintains it well, and also absorbs oil. If using a newly bought cast-iron pan, scrub it in soapy water, fill with leftover vegetables and water and bring to a boil. Discard and repeat 2–3 times and the iron odor will be removed.

Cast-iron pans are apt to produce metallic taste and rust. After each use, wash in soapy water using a sponge, and dry completely over heat. Rub a dab of oil over cooking surface and store in dry place.

Copper Pans

Copper pans conduct heat quickly and evenly. To prevent poisonous copper rust and surface oxidation, polish with vinegar and salt occasionally. Use a sponge for polishing, rinse with boiling water and wipe off moisture. This will bring back the copper shine. When rust appears, scrub with cleanser and rinse in lukewarm water.

Tin plating on cooking surface may come off after long time use. Have a specialist apply another plating.

Earthen Pots

Earthen Pots conduct heat gently but maintain it well, which is a great advantage in *nabemono* cooking. Despite the heavy appearance, earthen pots are very fragile. To prevent cracks, fill with heavily salted hot water and heat until the water decreases. Do not discard the water and allow to cool. Pour in hot water again and heat to boiling. This will make the pot durable for long time use.

When placing over heat, be sure to wipe off moisture from outside bottom and start with low heat. Do not put hot earthen pot into cold water.

If cracks appear, cook rice gruel in it and cracks will be sealed. If the bottom is burnt, do not scrub but pour in vinegar and water; heat for 10 minutes and then scrub. Wash after it is cooled, dry thoroughly and store in a dry place.

Shabu-shabu Pots

The roots of *shabu-shabu* come from a Chinese dish 'Peking Pot'. There are a great variety of *shabu-shabu* pots. Authentic pots have a center 'chimney' which hold charcoal or solid fuel. Another type is put on a gas or electric burner. It is made of brass, copper, or stainless steel. For home use, a sturdy stainless *shabu-shabu* pot is recommended. It is easy to look after. Electric skillets are good substitutes.

Iron Plates

An iron plate is placed on a direct heat and used to grill meats and vegetables. It maintains the heat very well and gives a sizzling sound, which creates the *teppanyaki* atmosphere. After each use, scrub in hot water and dry over heat; rub a dab of oil all over. If the corners are covered with burner grease, put over high heat to burn it into ash. Wash and dry over heat, rubbing a dab of oil all over. This will make the plate brand new.

Tempura Pans

Usually with side handles. Made of several materials. Cast-iron pans are most recommended because of heat maintainance.

Choose a deep pan with small diameter since the oil will oxidate on the surface. After each use, scrub in water and dry over heat.

Woks

There are round-bottomed and flat-bottomed, or one-handled and two-handled types. For home use, round bottomed ones with side handles are recommended. Materials should be cast-iron since stainless scorches easily and Teflon-coats are easily scarred. Cast-iron woks are multi-purpose pot; stir-frying, deep-frying, simmering and steaming with bamboo steamer.

Mini Shallow Frying Pans

Small one-handled pans used to make rice toppings individually. Usually made of aluminum; they are designed to fit the size of *donburi*, a large multi-purpose bowl, and to easily transfer onto rice. The topping can be slid smoothly onto the rice. No special seasoning is necessary.

Japanese Grinding Bowl

Pottery bowl serrated on the inside. It is useful when grinding small amounts of food such as sesame seeds, *tofu* or *miso* (soy bean paste). If using newly bought one, grind vegetable scraps to remove pottery powder between the grooves and to smooth the surface. After each use, wash with a brush, scrubbing along the grooves. Use bamboo skewer to remove tiny bits. Wipe off moisture and dry. When storing, do not place other ware on top to prevent abrasion.

Wooden Pestles

Used to grind food in grinding bowl. Choose one of firm wood such as Japanese pepper tree, and twice as long as the bowl diameter. Prior to use, soak in water and pat dry. This is to prevent sticking. After use, wash thoroughly and dry well.

Meat Pounders

Used to break down connective tissue of meat. They also level the thickness of meat, wrap and tap lightly with only this weight. They come in metallic, wooden, and plastic forms.

Graters

Graters come in red copper, aluminum, pottery, stainless and plastic forms. Tin-plated copper graters will last longer. After each use, wash under running water to remove tissues between 'teeth' and scrape off tiny tissues using a toothpick. To prevent rusting, scrub in vineger and salt mixture.

Colanders

Perforated utensils to drain food. Round stainless colanders are most popular and are used to sift dry ingredients or rinse off dirt or sand in water. Bamboo colanders have an advantage that they do not maintain the heat, and can be used to blanch in boiling water and cool at once. Be sure to remove dirt that is left in the mesh, using a brush. Store after drying thoroughly.

Baking Pans

Square shallow metallic containers. Many kinds of materials such as aluminum or enamel, sturdy stainless steel are recommended.
Uses are versatile; dividing ingredients, marinating, storing in refrigerator, or baking. Place a wire rack on it and use as an oil drainer for *tempura*. It is recommended to have different sizes.

Oil Strainers

Straining and storing into containers for frying oil. Usually made of stainless, it is often equipped with fine mesh. To clarify oil, strain through a paper towel to the mesh.

Sifters/Sieves

Best *tempura* batter is light and fluffy. By sifting flour the batter will contain air and become fluffy when deep-fried. After each use, clean the mesh carefully and dry thoroughly.

UTENSILS

Kitchen Thermometers

For home use there are two kinds, one for deep-frying and the other for oven cooking. Success of *tempura* lies in the oil temperature, so it is a good investment for light and crisp *tempura*. Look for one that can be attached to the frying pan for safety.

Skimmers

Fine netted stainless ladle to skim off splashes of batter while cooking *tempura*. It can be used to take *tempura* out. Other than *tempura*, use it to skim off residue or as a strainer. It easily gets greasy, so wash carefully using a brush.

Ladles

Deep-bowled, long-handled spoon used to dip out liquid. For pouring over sauces or skimming of fat or residue, use spout-type ladle. Round-bowl ladle holds approx ¾ cup 200cc, and spout-type ladle approx ⅓ cup 100cc, also they may be used as measuring cups!

Brushes

Brush to apply *teriyaki* sauce or egg yolk over grilled food. Made of animal hair or chemical fiber. In either case, wash and dry after each use. Since it is hard to remove the odor, keep it only for *teriyaki*.

Kitchen Scales

For home use, choose 5 lb/2 kg scales, with a large dish. Flat plates do not hold flour or nuts well. Do not leave things on the dish as it damages the spring.

Measuring Cups

1 cup is equivalent to 240 ml in this book. Usually made of glass, stainless or plastic. Stainless cups are most durable while glass ones are easy to read.

Measuring Spoons

There are four graduated sizes, tablespoon (T), teaspoon (t), half teaspoon (½t), and quarter teaspoon (¼t). 1 tablespoon is equivalent to 15 ml or 3 teaspoons. 1 teaspoon equals 5 ml. To measure dry ingredients, scoop into appropriate spoon until full, and level with a spatula/knife.

Microwave Ranges

For cooking foods speedily and cleanly. Without heating the utensils or oven, only the foods are heated. The food must contain moisture, and metal containers or china with metal decorations are not suitable (metals cause sparks). Microwaves do a good job in thawing frozen meats or poultry.

INGREDIENTS

BURDOCK ROOT

Burdock is on the market all year round, but it is best in early summer for its tenderness. Look for a thin, unbruised one. Full of vegetable tissue. Peel by scraping off skin using back of a knife. Season lightly since its rough consistency absorbs the taste well. Good for *nabemono* or *tempura*.

CHINESE CABBAGE

This versatile, greenish-white leafed cabbage is used in stir-fry and one-pot dishes. It is also added to soups, and made into pickles. A heavy, succulent vegetable, Chinese cabbage is often found in supermarkets, not to mention oriental food stores. It is also known as "celery cabbage" and "*nappa* (sometimes 'Napa') cabbage." Avoid produce with spotted leaves, if possible. Store as you would lettuce.

CHRYSANTHEMUM LEAVES

The perfume and blossoms of this vegetable are like chrysanthemums bred for garden display and cutting. But the edible foliage of the "spring" or "leaf" chrysanthemum are more deeply lobed and fuller than the decorative variety. The best ones are sold with roots attached. If you cannot obtain it, watercress or young spinach can be used as substitutes.

DAIKON RADISH

Daikon radish is otherwise known as icicle radish. It is rich in vitamins, and its leaves contain a lot of calcium. This radish is thought to aid in digesting oily foods. Good for simmered dishes.

DRIED BONITO

This is an important ingredient in *dashi* stock. A stick of dried bonito looks like a 6–8 in (15–20cm) long brownish hunk of wood.

Shaved, dried bonito flakes are also available in packs and convenient to use.

Dried bonito "thread" shavings are often used as a garnish. Such "thread" shavings look like rosy-beige excelsior and have a pleasant flavor. If you cannot obtain them, use regular dried bonito flakes.

EGGPLANTS

Eggplants used here are the 6 in (15cm) variety that weigh approximately 10 oz (285g) each, rather than the small Japanese eggplants that are on the average 4 in (10cm) long and weigh 2–3 oz (60–90g). Because size varies with region and season, weights have been included to offer a guideline. If using the small Japanese variety, substitute 3–4 eggplants in these recipes, again using the listed weight as a guide.

ENOKITAKE MUSHROOMS

Enokitake mushrooms are mild-flavored and have a pleasant crispness and aroma. They are often used in soups. There are canned *enokitake* mushrooms but fresh ones are better.

INGREDIENTS

GARLIC

Garlic is the pungent and strong-scented bulb of a European herb from the lily family. The stalks are also edible and can be used in stir-fried dishes.

Rich in glucide and vitamin B_1, garlic has a substance called arithin which unites with vitamin B_1 and prevents vitamin B_1 from destruction.

Although garlic is thought to be a food for stamina, it activates circulations and also stimulates the secretion of gastric juice. Therefore it is thought to be effective on colds, insomnia, parasites, neuralgia, muscular pains, and preventive for hardening arteries and high blood pressure.

It is said to work as a tranquilizer. Because of its strong effect on the body, overeating damages stomach and liver. Take a little amount regularly. Whole garlic marinated in soy sauce has less odor and is easy to eat.

GINGER ROOT

Ginger is a pungent, aromatic rootstalk of a genus Zingiber, tropical Asiatic and Polinesian herb. It is a popular spice all over the world.

The pungent substance promotes both appetite and digestion.

When using for stir-fried dishes, shred and cook in hot oil to extract the aroma. In this oil cook the other ingredients. Choose fresh root without wrinkles.

GREEN LAVER (*aonori*)

Flaked green laver is a popular garnish for many dishes. Rich in carotene and vitamin B_1 as well as calcium, phosphorus and iron. Especially iron content is higher than other seaweeds. If using a sheet type, toast very lightly. Overcooking will cause bitter taste.

GREEN ONION

The green onion referred to in this book is not the same as the green onion commonly found in U.S. markets. Substitutes are "leek", "scallion" and sometimes even "shallot".

GRILLED *TOFU*

Grilled *tofu* is called *yaki-dofu* in Japanese. Grilled *tofu* has been grilled on both sides over charcoal, thus producing its firm texture. It is easy to recognize by the light mottling on the skin. If *yaki-dofu* is not available, you can make it easily. Drain regular *tofu* and lightly grill each side of *tofu* over high heat. Grilled *tofu* is often used in boiled dishes such as *sukiyaki*.

JAPANESE CUCUMBER

Recipes in this book call for American cucumbers, which are equivalent to 2 or 3 Japanese cucumbers. In general, peel and seed cucumbers unless skin is delicate and thin and seeds are immature. If using the small Japanese variety, it is not necessary to peel or seed. However to smooth the rough surface and to bring out the skin color, dredge the cucumber in salt and roll it back and forth on a cutting board using the palm of your hand. Wash well.

KAMABOKO (steamed fish paste)

Kamaboko is made mainly from fish protein. Good *kamaboko* is white and elastic and the cut end is glossy. Keep in refrigerator.

INGREDIENTS

KONNYAKU STRIPS

Konnyaku, made from the roots of "devil's tongue" has no calories. It should be simmerd for a long time.

KOMBU KELP

Kombu is one of the basic ingredients used for making *dashi* stock. When you use it, never wash or rinse. The speckled surface of the kelp holds flavor, so do not wash. Kelp contains the most iodine of all seaweeds.

LOTUS ROOT

The flesh is white and "crunchy". Long tubular hollows run through the entire length of the root. When preparing lotus root for cooking, pare it first. Then cut into rounds. The shape should be attractive. To prevent discoloring it should be immersed for a short time in a mixture of alum and water or vinegar and water. This also gets rid of any harshness in flavor. It can then be boiled in water containing a little vinegar. It goes well with vinegared dishes.

MIRIN

Mirin is heavily sweetened *sake*, used for cooking. *Mirin* is also called "sweet cooking rice wine." It adds aroma and a touch of sweetness and is a basic seasoning in Japanese cooking.

MISO

Miso is fermented soybean paste. The colors range from yellow to brown; yellow *miso* is referred to as white *miso* in this book and brown *miso* as red *miso*. It might be helpful to learn about *miso* by buying small quantities of various kinds. It is used for soups, dressings, sauces, etc.

NORI SEAWEED

The best quality *nori* seaweed is glossy black-purple. It is used after toasting which improves flavor and texture. *Nori* seaweed grows around bamboo stakes placed under water. When the time comes, it is gathered, washed, laid in thin sheets and dried.

RICE

The rice that is preferred by Japanese people is short-grain rice. Short-grain rice is somewhat more glutinous than long-grain rice. The rice that Japanese people prefer is quite different from the one Western people think good. People in the West think rice should be dry and not sticky. The rice, which is dry like long-grain rice is not appropriate for Japanese cuisine, and should be avoided. Short-grain rice is always available in oriental food stores.

INGREDIENTS

RICE CAKE

Chewy *mochi* cakes are made by pounding hot steamed very glutinous rice in a barrel-sized wooden mortar with a large wooden mallet. Today, most *mochi* is machine processed and sold ready-made. The usual way of eating *mochi* is to grill it and eat with soy sauce or with a wrapper of toasted *nori* seaweed. When grilled, *mochi* will double in size, and a crisp skin will form. If *mochi* gets very hard and dry, it can be broken into small pieces and deep-fried. It will puff up in irregular shapes. Salted, these make a good snack.

SAKE

Sake is made by inoculating steamed mold (*koji*) and then allowing fermentation to occur. It is then refined it. In Japan *sake* is the most popular beverage, but it is also used in various ways for cooking.

SANSHO, KINOME SPRIGS

Both the leaves and seed pods of *sansho* are used. Dried leaves are powdered and used as a spice, *sansho* pepper. The young leaves, called *kinome* sprigs are mainly used to garnish foods.

SESAME OIL

Sesame oil is said to be the most aromatic of all oils. It is notable that because of the abundant vitamin E, it oxidizes very slowly, therefore it keeps well.

Sesame oil may sound Chinese, but it is an essential oil in Japanese cookery. Used in various ways such as stir-fried food, barbecue, and salad dressings. A sprinkling over the food just before serving adds a good flavor and gloss.

SESAME SEEDS

Sesame seeds are divided into three types; white, black, and yellow. Rich in lipids, white seeds are used to make sesame oil while strong-scented black seeds are used as a seasoning for rice or cakes. Aromatic yellow seeds are not produced enough for home use.

Lipids occupy more than half the content of sesame seeds, and are effective in preventing cholesterol from settling down. Therefore it is said to be a good food for preventing hardening of the arteries. Also protein makes up nearly 20% of the rest of the content. Calcium, iron, vitamin B_1, B_2, nicotinic acid are also good for preventing anemia and constipation.

Eaten in toasted or ground forms.

SHIITAKE MUSHROOMS

Both fresh and dried *shiitake* mushrooms can be obtained. Dried ones should be soaked in water before using. This soaking water makes *dashi* stock. Fresh *shiitake* mushrooms have a distinctive, appealing "woody-fruity" flavor. *Shiitake* mushrooms are good for simmered dishes because of their special flavor. The best ones have thick, brown velvety caps and firm flesh.

SHIMEJI MUSHROOMS

Fresh *shimeji* mushrooms should be delicately-crisp, and like *enokitake* mushroom in texture. The stems should be short and plump, and the flesh should be white. White mushrooms will do as a substitute if *shimeji* are not available.

INGREDIENTS

SHISO LEAVES

These minty, aromatic leaves come in green and red varieties. The red type is used to make *umeboshi* (pickled plum).

SOY SAUCE

Soy sauce is made from soy beans and salt. It is the primary seasoning in Japanese cooking. It is used for simmered foods, dressings, soups—many kinds of Japanese dishes. There are two kinds of soy sauce. One is ordinary soy sauce and the other is light soy sauce, which has a paler color and is less salty and does not darken the color of the foods. Soy sauce gives a delicate flavor and taste to foods.

TOFU

Tofu, "bean curd" in English, is an important product of soybeans. It is rich in proteins, vitamins, and minerals. It is low in calories and saturated fats, and entirely free of cholesterol.
There are two kinds of *tofu*: firm *tofu* and soft *tofu*.

TREFOIL

Trefoil is a member of the parsley family. The flavor is somewhere between sorrel and celery. The color of trefoil is light green and attractive. It is used in many Japanese dishes as a flavor and color accent. The leaves lose their fragrance easily so do not simmer too long or subject to too much heat.

UMEBOSHI (pickled plums)

Umeboshi are made every June when green plums come onto the market in Japan. Green, unripe plums are soaked in brine, packed with red *shiso* leaves and left to mature in the salty bath. In Japan *umeboshi* have long been regarded as a tonic. Not only are they thought to help in digestion, but they also keep the intestinal tract clear. This may be one of the reasons why *umeboshi* are served with the traditional Japanese breakfast. Also *umeboshi* paste can be used as a seasoning.

VINEGAR

Japanese rice vinegar is milder than most Western vinegars. Lightness and relative sweetness are characteristics of rice vinegar. Use cider vinegar rather than anything synthetic if substituting.

WAKAME SEAWEED

This seaweed is usually sold in dried form. *Wakame* seaweed can be used for various soups. It is also a good salad ingredient. It should not be simmered for more than a minute. *Wakame* seaweed is rich in vitamins and proteins.

YUZU CITRON

Japanese citron. The fragrant rind is grated and added as a garnish to soups and other dishes. This citrus fruit appears also in Chinese and Korean cooking. In the West where *yuzu* citron is not often available, lemon or lime rind or zest can be used though neither is quite the same.

METRIC TABLES

Today many areas of the world use the metric system and more will follow in the future. The following conversion tables are intented as a guide to help you.

General points of information that may prove valuable or of interest:
1 British fluid ounce = 28.5 ml
1 American fluid ounce = 29.5 ml

1 Japanese cup = 200 ml
1 British cup = 200 ml = 7 British fl oz
1 American cup = 240 ml = 8 American fl oz

1 British pint = 570 ml = 20 British fl oz
1 American pint = 470 ml = 16 American fl oz
T = tablespoon oz = ounce g = gram ml = milliliter

Weights

ounces to grams	grams to ounces
1/4 oz = 7 g	1 g = 0.035 oz
1/2 oz = 14 g	5 g = 1/6 oz
1 oz = 30 g	10 g = 1/3 oz
2 oz = 60 g	28 g ≒ 1 oz
4 oz = 115 g	100 g = 3 1/2 oz
6 oz = 170 g	200 g = 7 oz
8 oz = 225 g	500 g = 18 oz
16 oz = 450 g	1000 g = 35 oz

grams × 0.035 = ounces
ounces × 28.35 = grams

Linear Measures

inches to centimeters	centimeters to inches*
1/2 in = 1.27 cm	1 cm = 3/8 in
1 in = 2.54 cm	2 cm = 3/4 in
2 in = 5.08 cm	3 cm = 1 1/8 in
4 in = 10.16 cm	4 cm = 1 1/2 in
5 in = 12.7 cm	5 cm = 2 in
10 in = 25.4 cm	10 cm = 4 in
15 in = 38.1 cm	15 cm = 5 3/4 in
20 in = 50.8 cm	20 cm = 8 in

inches × 2.54 = centimeters
centimeters × 0.39 = inches

in = inch   cm = centimeter

Temperature

Fahrenheit (F) to Celsius (C)		Celsius (C) to Fahrenheit (F)	
freezer storage	−10°F = −23.3°C	freezer storage	−20°C = −4°F
	0°F = −17.7°C		−10°C = 14°F
water freezes	32°F = 0 °C	water freezes	0°C = 32°F
	68°F = 20 °C		10°C = 50°F
	100°F = 38 °C		50°C = 122°F
water boils	212°F = 100 °C	water boils	100°C = 212°F
	300°F = 150 °C		150°C = 302°F
	400°F = 204.4°C		200°C = 392°F

The water boiling temperatu given is at sea level.

Conversion factors:

$$C = \frac{(F - 32) \times 5}{9}$$

$$F = \frac{C \times 9}{5} + 32$$

C = Celsius   F = Fahrenheit

INDEX